1. Trace the pattern on the dull side of freezer paper.

2. Iron freezer paper onto fabric, shiny side down. Cut out pieces.

3. Pin or baste wool shapes in place.

4. Applique wool shapes in place using Perle cotton and a Blanket stitch.

5. Layer the backing, the batting and the top of the table runner; baste in place.

6. Outline quilt around appliques.

7. Fold binding to back of quilt.

8. Stitch in the ditch to secure binding.

You'll find a handy stitch guide on page 98. Have fun!

January

Snowflakes are falling...

The snowflake is one of nature's most fragile creations, but look what they can do when they stick together!

After you shovel the mounds of snowflakes out of your driveway, gather your friends in a warm sewing room and "stitch together". You can make just one project, or make it a date to meet each month and make the quilt! You will be amazed at how fast the work goes in the company of friends.

Snowflakes Table Runner

Do you remember the cut out snowflakes you made in school? We decorated our classroom windows with them, and then carried them home to adorn the windows in our bedrooms. This table runner will warm your heart with memories of a simpler time.

see patterns on page 32 & 33

Snowflakes Pincushion

Pretty enough to set on a dressing table, this pincushion is the perfect place to store the pins and needles. Great Grandma would have kept her hat pins here.

see patterns on page 32 & 33

Snowflakes Needle Case

Keep track of needles in this felted wool ornamental book. Needles won't rust because wool is a natural fiber that doesn't hold moisture.

see patterns on page 32 & 33

Sweethearts Coasters

Don't these little coasters remind you of Linzer tortes? Set a holiday mood with these heart-shaped coasters. Label them with the words from conversation candy hearts...just for fun!

see patterns on page 36

Sweetie's House Slippers

Here's a wonderful gift idea. Personalize the hearts on these sweet slippers with an embroidery design or an initial. It is easier if you think of this before the hearts are attached to the slippers! It will warm your heart to see someone you love enjoy this fancy footwear and keep their toes warm too!

see patterns on page 35

Heart Pin Pincushion

"Ever since I began to sew I have been sticking pins into my shirts. I didn't like the feel of a wrist pincushion on my arm, and the ring pincushions were just too large. While working on this book I found myself doing it again. Actually, I was being teased about the pins in my shirt when a bright idea hit me. Make a pin that doubles as a pincushion. This just makes good sense! If not used as a pincushion, it is still cute enough to wear as a piece of jewelry or special enough to give to a person who collects pincushions!"

- Betty Edgell

see patterns on page 35

February

The Queen of Hearts...

Cupid's Arrow Runner

Arrows and hearts create a romantic runner for your Valentine evening meal.

see patterns on page 37

Jewelry Pincushion

Set this heart pincushion on your dresser to showcase your favorite jewelry pins.

see patterns on page 34

Morning Glory Penny Rug

It's March and there may still be snow on the ground where you live, but the flowers are beginning to break through the earth.

Decorate your table with a wish for warmer days as lovely morning glories grace this snow-white background made from felted wool.

see patterns on page 40

Morning Glory Pillowcase

Remember the warm, clean feeling of pillowcases dried on the clothesline? Bring a bit of spring into a room with this pillowcase decorated with morning glories.

see patterns on page 39

Morning Glory Table Runner

It's March and spring is just around the corner. Capture a ray of sunshine with a beautiful yellow fabric. Get your garden growing with this lovely array of morning glories. Made in blue, these appliques are such a welcome surprise. Whether climbing happily through your garden gate or bringing some springtime to the table, these lovely flowers will always make you smile.

see patterns on page 39

 **arch**

Spring and new beginnings...

Bunny Hop...

Spring bonnets...

Time to hunt the eggs...

Bunny Hop Table Runner

Bunnies are a favorite Spring motif. This one is easy enough to finish in a weekend, so you will still have time to get the frills on your Easter bonnet.

see patterns on pages 41 & 42

Bunny Hop To It Tea Towel

Make a few "Hop To It" tea towels and keep them near the children's table so those little spills don't become a big a mess at your Easter gathering.

see patterns on page 42

Easter Coasters

Greet your Easter guests with a cool glass of pink lemonade and a cheerful coaster in pastel Easter egg colors and shapes.

see patterns on page 43

Get your Spring bonnet...

"They are out of their cage again! Basil and Suzy, fluffy white bunnies with bright eyes, were given as Easter gifts to my brother Bobby and me in the early 1960's. Bobby was fascinated with Mark Wilson, the magician, and hoped to become a magician as well. Bobby planned to pull Basil out of a hat. I was his assistant. Little did we know just how magical Basil and Suzy were! They continually disappeared from their cage, causing us to search all over for them."

- Betsy Chutchian

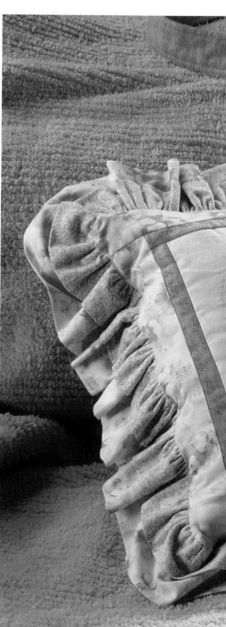

Cozy Posy House Slippers

Remember how much Mom loves flowers? Give her posies for her toes this Mother's Day. These comfortable slippers in pretty spring colors are sure to please.

see patterns on page 45

Cozy Posy Tea Cozy

Revive the British custom of "afternoon tea". It's a great excuse to get out your best tea set, have some scones with friends, and show off your Posy Cozy. Make several for gifts and you will have the upcoming bridal shower covered.

see patterns on page 45

Pot o' Posies Table Runner

April showers bring May flowers. And here they are! Judith Lester showers you with six Posy projects fit for Mother's Day gifts, birthday presents or home decor. With a bolster for your head, and slippers for your toes, she has this month covered. Spend an afternoon with your niece or granddaughter learning to embroider the posy basket pillow. Or gather your quilting group and share some tea under the Posy Cozy. The table runner truly "ties up" this set of projects with its beautiful bow and baskets of flowers.

see patterns on page 44 - 46

May

May flowers bring pretty posies!

Posy Basket Pillows & Bolster

If you love embroidery, this project is for you! Choose beautiful ruffle fabrics for the pillow and coordinate your threads for an attractive home decor project you will proudly display on your sofa or bed.

Create a bolster that is a simple tube with ribbon ties. It's a great project for a youth group, since it only requires inexpensive supplies, and it offers an opportunity to learn basic sewing and applique skills.

see patterns on pages 45 - 46

 # June

Let's have a picnic...

Melon Pincushion

A perfect gift for anyone who sews, this bright reminder of summer days will hold your pins as you quilt through the cold months of winter.

see patterns on page 52

Melon Eyeglasses Case

Enjoy the sights of summer and keep your sunglasses close at hand in a case that celebrates a seasonal favorite.

see patterns on page 51

Melon Checkbook Cover

Get your checkbook and go marketing. Pick up summer's best flavors at your local farmer's market.

see patterns on page 51

Watermelon Table Runner

It's June. The kids are out of school. The weather is warm. Baseball season is under way. It's time for that picnic at the park. Use this Watermelon Table Runner to set the picnic table and enjoy a sunny afternoon with family and friends.

see patterns on pages 48 - 50

# July

Vacations, reunions, quilting at the beach...

Hollyhocks Table Runner

The delicate flowers of spring have faded into memory, replaced by summer's sun-loving, hearty varieties. Judith Lester has picked her favorite hollyhocks to decorate this month's dining table. Prefer your flowers "to go"? Make up the Hollyhocks Tote bag.

see patterns on pages 54 & 55

Hollyhocks Tote Bag

Whether you are going to the beach, on vacation, or just to the grocery store, tote bags always come in handy. Make this pretty one in a jiffy with pink buttons and scraps of wool. The basket weave fabric is the perfect canvas for your art.

see patterns on page 53

Sunflowers in a Rusty Bucket Table Runner

"This table runner reminds me of the time I saw the county mower coming toward my house. The sunflowers growing just on the other side of our property line were about to be whacked down. In a rush, I grabbed a shovel and the only 2 buckets I could find. I quickly dug up the defenseless flowers and got them safely before the mower came. In gratitude, they grew happily in their buckets all summer, generously donating their seeds to the neighborhood birds." — Judith Lester

see patterns on pages 58 & 59

Sunny Table Linens

Decorate your patio table with this simple yet elegant table covering. The matching napkins complete the ensemble. Set the table with yellow dishes, and you will be ready for a candlelight dinner, or luncheon with friends.

see patterns on page 57

August

The last flowers of summer...

There is nothing like doing needlework in the sunshine. You get perfect light, and because you are relaxed, your stitches are probably more even than usual.

Sunflower Needle Case

Everyone who sews has needles, and needs to keep them handy. Make a pretty case that will be easy to find in your sewing basket.

see patterns on page 56

Blooming Pincushion

Keep your pins from rusting and lift your spirits at the same time. Sunflowers always look up at the sun. They remind us to do the same. Keep smiling.

see patterns on page 56

September

The falling leaves...

"Fall is my favorite time of the year. Autumn has aromas and sounds uniquely its own. I love the rainbow of color in falling leaves. I love raking leaves, and leaping into them. I'll never forget the way they smell and the way they crunch under my shoes.

Like the squirrels, I collect bits of fall. I still pick up a few acorns. I still press leaves. I have carefully preserved chestnuts in small jars beside my buttons. These bits inspire me with their rustic textures as I work on my sewing and choose fabrics for my quilts."

- Betty Edgell

Welcome Penny Rug

"September is the Hazel month in the old Celtic calendar. Its color is brown. It is a time of gathering fruitfulness and hospitality. This project explodes with all my favorite things, warmly welcoming friends to celebrate a season of resplendent color. We renew old friendships and plan new quilts over steaming mugs of cider. Energy is high, as we prepare for a winter of sewing."

- Betty Edgell

see patterns on pages 60 & 61

"Leaf Through a Book" Bookmark

As the days get shorter and cooler, there are fewer chores to do in the yard. It's time to settle down with your favorite quilting book and start planning projects for Christmas. Mark your place with this pretty leaf. Then, go to your sewing room and make several stocking stuffers for all the book lovers in your family. Do it now, and avoid the Christmas rush.

see pattern on page 61

Flying South Table Runner

The summer birds are gathering for their flight to warmer climates. Leaves gently drift from a sky of flying geese in this beautifully executed artwork. Let this project bring the joy of life's journey to your table.

see patterns on pages 60 & 61

October

It's the great pumpkin...

Matt's Cat in the Pumpkin Patch Table Runner

"In the summer of 2002, my son Matt appeared with this beautiful black kitten. 'Mom, I'm keeping him,' he declared. By the look on his face, I knew Matt was in love with this cat. By fall, Winston was officially a member of the family, much to the dismay of our other cats, Bandit and Shadow. Winston leaps, jumps, and runs throughout the house as he and Matt play chase, convinced that Matt is a cat."

- Betsy Chutchian

see patterns on pages 63 - 69

Pumpkin Place Mats

Add a seasonal touch to your table with these eye-catching place mats. Use them at the Halloween party and for the Thanksgiving feast… two for one!

see patterns on page 66

Pumpkin Pincushion

Did you know that collectors look for unusual pincushions? This Pumpkin Pincushion is perfect for the friend who loves fall, pumpkins, Halloween and pincushions!

see patterns on page 69

ovember

Harvest Time...

Pineapple Tea Cozy

Pineapples were originally a sign of affluence and hospitality, so pamper your guests with some exotic tastes and serve an afternoon tea in style with this Pineapple Tea Cozy.

see patterns on page 72

Pineapple Bread Cloth

A tempting array of delicious fresh breads deserves a proper presentation. Make this Pineapple Bread Cloth to complete your table theme. And while you're at it, make a couple for hostess gifts so you have them on hand for all those upcoming holiday parties.

see patterns on page 73

Pineapple Table Runner

What month could be more welcoming than the one in which we celebrate Thanksgiving? Surprise your dinner guests with an out-of-the-ordinary motif that symbolizes hospitality. Make this beautiful table runner, and complete your table decor with the bread cloth and tea cozy. Top it off with a real pineapple centerpiece for an elegant and memorable table setting.

see patterns on pages 70 & 71

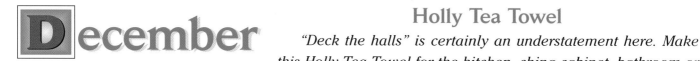

December

It's beginning to look a lot like Christmas...

Holly Berry Slippers

Warm hands, warm hearts, warm nose, warm toes! Stuff everyone's stocking with these comfortable, easy-to-make slippers.

see patterns on page 75

Holly Penny Rug

Add a bit of holiday cheer to the coffee table with this fun Holly Penny Rug.

see patterns on page 76 & 77

Holly Tea Towel

"Deck the halls" is certainly an understatement here. Make this Holly Tea Towel for the kitchen, china cabinet, bathroom or guest room.

see patterns on page 75

Holly Table Runner

"The creamy background of the table runner reminds me of the special cakes my grandmothers made for Christmas. Grandmother Carter made a fresh coconut cake. She roasted the coconut, cracked it open with a hammer and grated the delectable coconut to coat a seven-minute icing.

Grandmother Reed also made a special cake. Her famous Japanese Fruitcake was a complicated concoction of seven white layers and a gooey filling and topping of pineapple, cherries, oranges, raisins and pecans in a custard-like base. Soon after assembly the cake would always fall apart. The appearance made no difference to my grandfather, who always ate half the cake before dinner!"

- Betsy Chutchian

see patterns on pages 74 & 75

Seasonal Delights Quilt

Life is a celebration to be cherished. You have spent time each month preparing the motifs for this quilt. Now, it is time to enjoy putting them together. Relax while you quilt. Savor the experience as you stitch the binding in place. Chat with friends as you attach the label to your masterpiece. Then, put on your Christmas slippers, pack your needles in their assorted needle cases, brew a pot of tea under the Posy Cozy, put the pins back in their pincushions and RELAX with friends. Look back on a wonderful year of completed gifts, useful home decorations and your newest quilted creation.

see patterns on pages 78 - 97

January Table Runner

by Judith Lester

Finished size: 15¹/2" x 43¹/2"

MATERIALS:
- Background: ¹/8 yd each of 5 shades of Blue (4¹/2" x 45")
- Border: 1 yd
- Binding: ¹/3 yard (9" x 45")
- Backing: 18" x 47"
- Batting: 18" x 47"
- White felted wool 14" x 19"
- *DMC* size 8 Pale Blue Perle cotton for hand applique and size 8 Ecru Perle cotton for hand quilting
- Fusible web for snowflakes

INSTRUCTIONS:

1. Cut 30 Blue 4¹/2" squares from the background strips. Cut 2 long Blue borders 2" x 40¹/2". • Cut 2 side Blue borders 2" x 15¹/2". Cut 4 strips of binding 2¹/2" x width of fabric.

2. Arrange the squares in a pleasing manner 10 across, 3 down. Use ¹/4" seams to sew the squares together. Press the seams in the first row to the right. Press the seams in the second row to the left. Press the seams in the third row to the right. Sew the rows together. Add the long borders. Press the seams toward the border. Add the short border. Press the seams toward the border.

3. Trace snowflakes onto the paper side of fusible web. Following manufacturer's directions, fuse White wool to the web. Cut out snowflakes. Arrange snowflakes on pieced top. It is recommended that you fuse and stitch one snowflake at a time. Hand or machine applique snowflakes to top.

4. Layer the backing, batting, and top. Baste layers together. Hand or machine quilt as desired.

5. Sew the binding strips together. Fold and press so you have a piece 1¹/4" x 180". Sew binding to quilt using a ¹/4" seam. Fold the binding over and sew down by hand or machine.

There are 5 different fabrics used in the January Table Runner shown here in shades of gray.

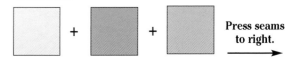

1. First Row

Press seams to right.

2. Second Row

Press seams to the left.

3. Third Row

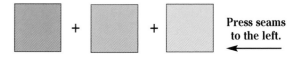

Press seams to right.

4. Sew the rows together.

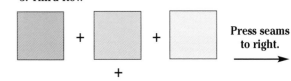

Continued on page 35

Patterns for Table Runner on pages 32 & 33.

Snowflake Needle Case

by Judith Lester

Finished size: 3" x 4"

MATERIALS:
- Blue felted wool (3" x 8¹/4")
- 2 pieces White felted wool (2³/4" x 7¹/2")
- White felted wool for snowflake (2¹/2" square)
- 2 pieces White satin ribbon 8" long
- *DMC* size 8 Pale Blue Perle cotton
- Fusible web for snowflake
- Small embroidery scissors

INSTRUCTIONS:

1. Choose a snowflake pattern from January Snowflake Table Runner. Trace snowflake onto the paper side of fusible web. Following manufacturer's directions, fuse White wool to the web. Cut out snowflake. Fuse snowflake to the Blue wool. • 2. Use a Blanket stitch and Perle cotton to applique snowflake. • 3. Stitch a ribbon to each end of the Blue wool to tie closed. • 4. To form the inside of the book, sew one White wool rectangle to the Blue wool ¹/8" from the edge with a Running stitch. • 5. Place the second White wool over the first. Fold like a book. Crease or mark the fold. Sew the layers together along the fold line with a Running stitch. • 6. Sew a Blanket stitch around the outside edge of the Blue wool.

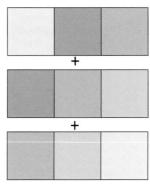

SNOWFLAKE NEEDLE CASE PATTERN

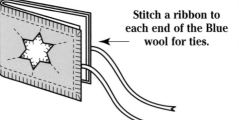

Stitch a ribbon to each end of the Blue wool for ties.

Tie ribbon in a bow to close.

5. Make snowflakes and applique to pieced top.
6. Add the long borders.
Press the seams toward the border.

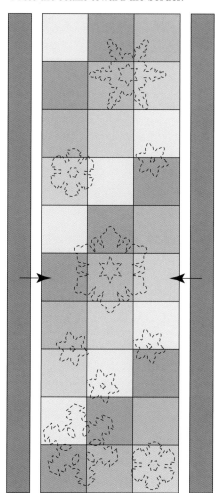

7. Add the short borders.
Press the seams toward the border.

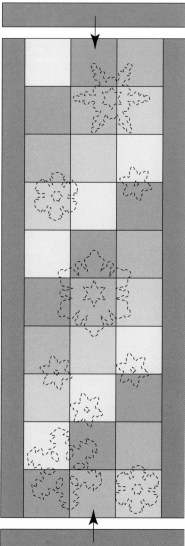

8. Sew binding to edges by hand or with machine.

Snowflake Pincushion

by Judith Lester

Finished size: $5^1/2$" x $5^1/2$"

MATERIALS:
- 2 pieces Blue felted wool $5^1/2$" x $5^1/2$"
- 1 piece White felted wool $5^1/2$" x $5^1/2$"
- *DMC* size 8 Pale Blue Perle cotton for hand applique
- Fusible web for snowflakes
- Wool or cotton stuffing (so the pins won't rust)

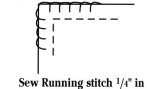

Sew Running stitch $^1/4$" in around 3 sides of pincushion. Stuff and close opening with Running stitch. To finish, Blanket stitch around edges of pincushion.

INSTRUCTIONS:

1. Choose a snowflake pattern from January Snowflake Table Runner. Trace snowflake onto paper side of fusible web. • 2. Following manufacturer's directions, fuse White wool to web. Cut out snowflake. Fuse snowflake to the Blue wool. • 3. Use Blanket stitch and Perle cotton to applique snowflake. • 4. Place the second Blue square behind appliqued square. Use Running stitch to sew around 3 sides $^1/4$" from edge. Stuff and close opening with a Running stitch. • 5. Blanket stitch around the edge.

TABLE RUNNER
and
PINCUSHION PATTERN

This may be
used as an
APPLIQUE
PATTERN
when cut out.

Snowflakes

Photos on pages 4 - 5

This may be used as an APPLIQUE PATTERN when cut out.

SNOWFLAKE PATTERNS

Place on Fold and cut out for complete pattern.

When unfolded, your pattern will look like this.

 # February

Photo on page 7

Jewelry Pincushion
by Betty Edgell

Finished size: 7" x 10"

MATERIALS:
- Red felted wool (10" x 18")
- 1 Ecru felted wool 8" square
- 1 yd. of 3/4" wide Ecru crocheted cotton scalloped lace
- 1 yd. of 5/8" wide Ecru satin ribbon
- 4" piece of 5/8" wide Ecru lace ribbon
- Natural wool or cotton fiber stuffing
- Ecru sewing thread
- *DMC* size 8 Perle cotton (Ecru & Red) or *DMC* embroidery floss to match

INSTRUCTIONS:
1. Trace the large and medium hearts onto freezer paper. Cut out paper hearts.
2. Press large heart pattern on Red wool. Cut out 2 hearts.
3. Press medium pattern on White wool. Cut out 1 heart.
4. Arrange the lace around and under the White heart. Baste the lace in place.
5. Fold back 1/4" at each end of the lace ribbon. Pin the ribbon across one side of the White heart as shown in the photo. Sew lace in place. Add additional embellishments if desired.
6. Center the White heart on one Red heart and pin in place. Use Ecru Perle cotton and a Blanket stitch to sew hearts together.
7. Place the decorated Red heart on top of the remaining Red heart and Blanket stitch around the outer edges, leaving a 2" opening.
8. Stuff pincushion. Blanket stitch opening closed.
9. Locate center of satin ribbon. Stitch center of ribbon in place. Tie the ribbon in a bow.

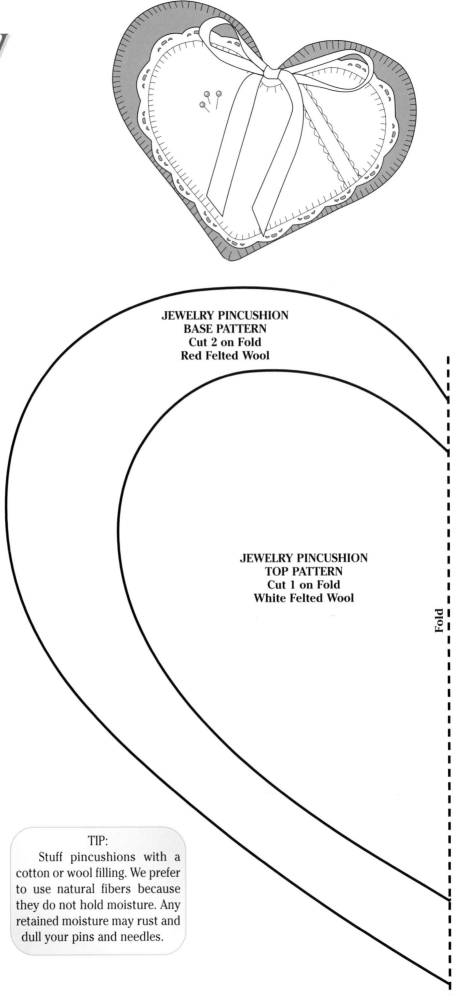

JEWELRY PINCUSHION
BASE PATTERN
Cut 2 on Fold
Red Felted Wool

JEWELRY PINCUSHION
TOP PATTERN
Cut 1 on Fold
White Felted Wool

Fold

TIP:
Stuff pincushions with a cotton or wool filling. We prefer to use natural fibers because they do not hold moisture. Any retained moisture may rust and dull your pins and needles.

Heart Pin Pincushion

by Betty Edgell

Finished Size: $4^1/2$" x $3^1/2$"

MATERIALS:
- Red felted wool (8" square)
- White felted wool (3" x 3")
- *DMC* Red size 8 Perle cotton or embroidery floss
- Natural wool or cotton fiber stuffing
- 1" jewelry back pin
- Hot glue

INSTRUCTIONS:

1. Trace heart patterns on freezer paper. Press large heart pattern and heart with a hole on Red wool. Cut out both hearts.

2. Cut a piece of White wool and position it under the cut out section of Red heart.

3. Use Red pearl cotton or 2 strands of Red embroidery floss to Blanket stitch around the inside edge to join the top to the White heart.

4. Attach the Red and White small heart to the bottom Red heart with a Blanket stitch around the outer edge of the Red and White top heart.

5. Join the two base hearts with a Blanket stitch, leaving a 2" opening. Stuff the base lightly with wool or cotton fibers. Buttonhole stitch the opening closed.

6. Attach the pin back to the heart with hot glue or sewing thread.

Sweetie's House Slippers

by Betty Edgell

MATERIALS:
- 1 pair of purchased Pink slippers
- Red or Pink felted wool (5" square)
- 2 pieces of *Offray* Bright Pink $1/4$" wide satin ribbon 10" long
- Two 1" heart charms
- *DMC* size 8 Perle cotton or embroidery floss to match wool
- Large eye sharp needle

INSTRUCTIONS:

1. Draw 4 heart patterns on freezer paper. Iron patterns onto felt. Cut out hearts. Peel off paper.

2. Use pearl cotton or 2 strands of embroidery floss to secure hearts to the slippers with blanket stitches as shown in the photo or in a design you prefer.

3. Use a large needle to thread ribbon through slipper at the top dip of one heart. Pull ribbon ends even and thread one charm onto one end. Tie ribbon in a bow to secure the charm in place. Repeat for other slipper.

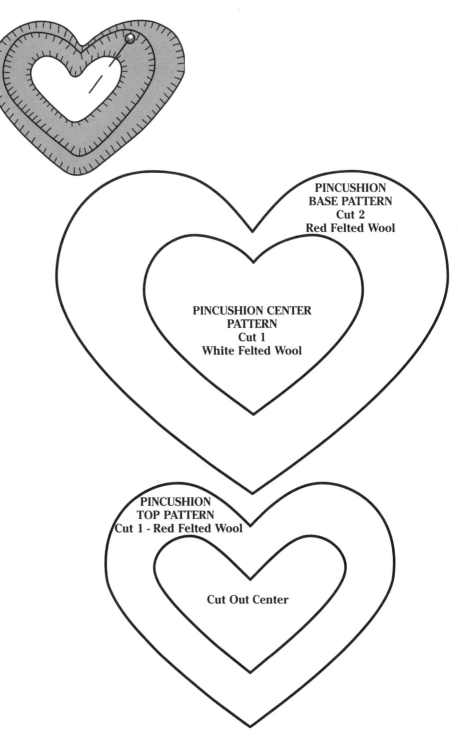

PINCUSHION BASE PATTERN
Cut 2
Red Felted Wool

PINCUSHION CENTER PATTERN
Cut 1
White Felted Wool

PINCUSHION TOP PATTERN
Cut 1 - Red Felted Wool

Cut Out Center

Use the little Red heart centers you cut out for the coasters to make the Sweetie's House Slippers.

SLIPPERS PATTERN
Cut 4
Red Felted Wool

February

Photo on page 6

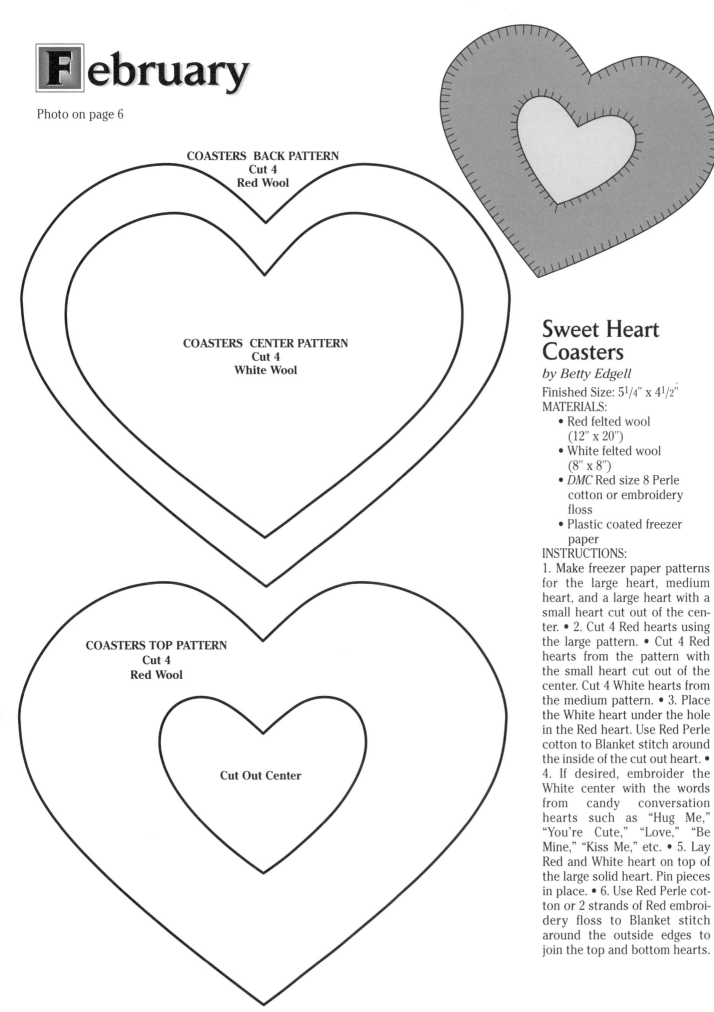

COASTERS BACK PATTERN
Cut 4
Red Wool

COASTERS CENTER PATTERN
Cut 4
White Wool

COASTERS TOP PATTERN
Cut 4
Red Wool

Cut Out Center

Sweet Heart Coasters

by Betty Edgell

Finished Size: 5$^{1}/4$" x 4$^{1}/2$"

MATERIALS:
- Red felted wool (12" x 20")
- White felted wool (8" x 8")
- *DMC* Red size 8 Perle cotton or embroidery floss
- Plastic coated freezer paper

INSTRUCTIONS:
1. Make freezer paper patterns for the large heart, medium heart, and a large heart with a small heart cut out of the center. • 2. Cut 4 Red hearts using the large pattern. • Cut 4 Red hearts from the pattern with the small heart cut out of the center. Cut 4 White hearts from the medium pattern. • 3. Place the White heart under the hole in the Red heart. Use Red Perle cotton to Blanket stitch around the inside of the cut out heart. • 4. If desired, embroider the White center with the words from candy conversation hearts such as "Hug Me," "You're Cute," "Love," "Be Mine," "Kiss Me," etc. • 5. Lay Red and White heart on top of the large solid heart. Pin pieces in place. • 6. Use Red Perle cotton or 2 strands of Red embroidery floss to Blanket stitch around the outside edges to join the top and bottom hearts.

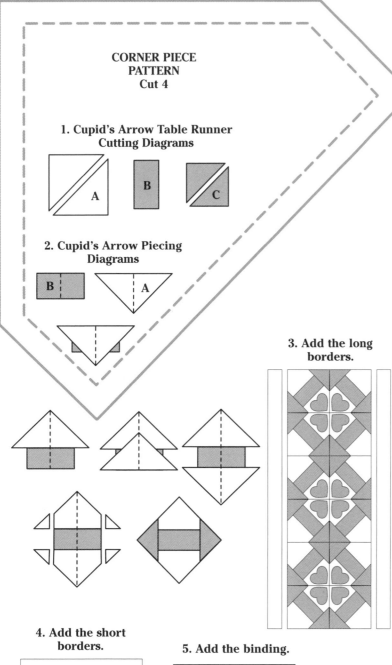

CORNER PIECE PATTERN Cut 4

1. Cupid's Arrow Table Runner Cutting Diagrams

A   B   C

2. Cupid's Arrow Piecing Diagrams

B   A

3. Add the long borders.

4. Add the short borders.

5. Add the binding.

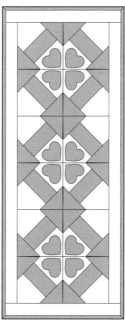

HEART PATTERN Cut 16 Red wool

Cupid's Arrows Table Runner

by Betty Edgell

Finished Size: 15$\frac{1}{2}$" x 39"

MATERIALS:
- Background: $\frac{5}{8}$ yd Ecru
- Design Prints: 12 assorted Red fabrics (10$\frac{1}{2}$" x 10$\frac{1}{2}$")
- Border: $\frac{1}{2}$ yd Cream
- Binding: $\frac{1}{4}$ yd makes 3 Red strips (2$\frac{1}{2}$" x 45")
- Backing: $\frac{1}{2}$ yd Cream with Red stars
- Batting: 18" x 42"
- Red felted wool 12" x 12"
- *DMC* Ecru and Red size 8 Perle cotton or embroidery floss
- Plastic coated freezer paper

INSTRUCTIONS:

1. Cut 12 Ecru 5$\frac{1}{2}$" squares. Cut each square in half diagonally. (A)   Cut backing 18" x 42" across the width of the fabric. From each Red Design print, cut 1 rectangle 2$\frac{1}{2}$" x 4$\frac{3}{4}$" (B) and 1 square 3$\frac{7}{8}$". Cut each square in half diagonally. (C)

2. Use $\frac{1}{4}$" seam allowances throughout.

3. Piece together according to the diagram. Fold each solid Red rectangle (B) in half. Finger press. Fold each Ecru triangle (A) in half. Finger press. With right sides together, match the centers and sew the long side. Open the pieces and press seam to the dark fabric. Repeat with another Ecru triangle (A) on the other side of the rectangle. Trim the fabric even at each side.

4. With right sides facing, sew a Red triangle (C) to each side of the piece. Open the piece and press seams to one side. Trim block to 6$\frac{1}{2}$" square. Repeat to make 12 blocks.

5. Lay out blocks in the design shown. Sew 2 blocks together to form a row. Press seams in opposite directions for each row. Sew 6 rows together.

6. Cut 2 long Ecru borders 2" x 36$\frac{1}{2}$". Sew to both sides. Press toward border. Cut 2 short Ecru borders 2" x 15$\frac{1}{2}$". Sew to both sides. Press seams toward border.

7. Draw heart patterns on freezer paper. Iron patterns onto wool. Cut hearts out on line. Peel off paper. Use Red pearl cotton or 2 strands of Red embroidery floss and Blanket stitch the wool hearts to the quilt top as shown.

8. Layer the backing, batting and the assembled top. Center the top, right side up, on the batting. Baste all the layers together.

9. Quilt as desired with Ecru Perle cotton or 3 strands of floss. Remove the basting stitches. Trim the batting even with the edges of the quilt top.

10. Cut 3 strips of Red print 2$\frac{1}{2}$" x width of fabric and bind the edges with the strips.

Morning Glory Table Runner

by Betsy Chutchian

Finished Size: $16^1/2$" x $40^1/2$"

MATERIALS:

- Background: $1/4$ yd each of 5 soft Yellow fabrics and $1/3$ yd Dark Gold tone on tone fabric (12" x 45")
- Border: $1/4$ yd Gold Marble
- Binding: $1/4$ yd Yellow check
- Backing: $1/2$ yd Yellow check
- Batting: (18" x 45")
- Mottled Light Blue felted wool (10" x 12")
- Green felted wool or Green cotton for vines (18" x 22")
- Green felted wool in a different shade than the vines (6" x 12")
- 1 skein each of *DMC* size 8 Perle cotton (Yellow #3823, Light Gray #415, Green #94 and #937) or embroidery floss.
- Plastic coated freezer paper

INSTRUCTIONS:

1. From 5 soft Yellow fabrics and the Dark Gold, cut 14 squares $4^7/8$". • 2. Layer a Dark Gold square on top of a soft Yellow square, right sides together. Draw a line on the diagonal. Sew $1/4$" on each side of the line. Cut on the diagonal line. Press seams to the darker fabric. Trim to $4^1/2$". You need 27 half-square triangles. • 3. Sew the half-square triangles in a Broken Dishes set, 3 rows of 9. (See diagram.) • 4. Cut 2 Gold borders $2^1/2$" x $36^1/2$". Add long borders. Press toward the border. Cut 2 Gold borders $2^1/2$" x $16^1/2$". Add short borders. Press toward the border. • 5. Layer top, batting, and backing. Baste. Quilt with Yellow Perle cotton. (See diagram.) •

6. Prepare appliques: Cut narrow bias strips from Green wool $1/4$" or from cotton $3/4$" to finish at $1/4$". Trace shapes on freezer paper and cut out on drawn line. Press shiny side of freezer paper onto wool. Cut out 10 flowers and 13 leaves. • 7. Arrange applique pieces as shown in photo. • 8. Using a Blanket stitch, applique flowers and leaves. Use a Running stitch down the center of the wool vines to hold them in place. If you use cotton vines, Blind stitch or Blanket stitch both sides. Embroider details in flowers and leaves with a Stem stitch or Backstitch. Make French Knots at the end of the stamens. • 9. Cut 3 binding strips $2^1/2$" wide. Join the strips end to end. Fold with raw edges together. Stitch binding in place.

1. How to Make Half Square Triangles

4. Add the appliques and binding.

2. Add the long borders.

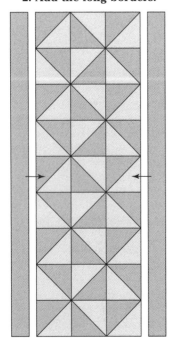

3. Add the short borders.

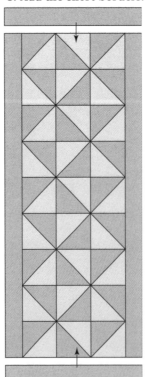

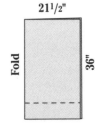
**MORNING GLORY
PATTERNS**

Morning Glories Pillowcase

by Betsy Chutchian

Finished Size: standard size 21" x 30$\frac{1}{2}$"

MATERIALS:

- 1 yd Gold check fabric for pillowcase
- Mottled Medium Blue felted wool (6" x 6")
- Olive Green felted wool (4" x 6")
- *DMC* Light Blue and Light Olive size #8 Perle cotton or embroidery floss
- 24" long bias strip of $\frac{1}{4}$" wide Green felted wool or $\frac{3}{4}$" wide Green cotton
- Plastic coated freezer paper

INSTRUCTIONS:

1. Trim away selvages on pillowcase fabric to make fabric. Mark these edges for reference later. • 2. With right sides facing out, fold marked edges together to 21$\frac{1}{2}$" x 36". • 3. Center and mark applique placement according to diagram. • 4. If using cotton for stem, make Green bias by folding both edges under. Press. Or use wool bias strip for stem. Trace flowers and leaves on freezer paper and transfer onto wool. Cut out 3 flowers and 3 leaves. • 5. Using a Blanket stitch, applique flowers and leaves. Use a Running stitch down the center of the wool vines. If you use cotton vines, Blind stitch or Blanket stich both sides. Embroider details in flowers and leaves with a Stem stitch or Backstitch. Make French Knots at the end of the stamens. • 6. Fold pillowcase with right sides together. Sew end and side seams. (See diagram). •
7. Fold up $\frac{1}{2}$" on open end. Press. Fold up a 4" hem. Press. Pin in place. Topstitch continuously around the cuff, close to the hem edge. Turn the pillowcase right side out. Press well.

Making the Pillowcase

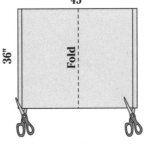

45"

36"

Fold

Trim away selvages on pillowcase fabric.

21$\frac{1}{2}$"

Fold

36"

With right sides facing out, fold marked edges together to 21$\frac{1}{2}$" x 36". Stitch applique 4$\frac{1}{2}$" from edge.

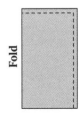

Fold

Fold pillowcase with right sides together. Sew end and side seams.

Morning Glories Penny Rug

by Betsy Chutchian

Finished Size: 17" x 17"

MATERIALS:
- Background: Ecru coat weight felted wool (11"square)
- Design Prints: Mottled Light Blue felted wool (8" x 12")
- Backing: Blue and White homespun cotton (13" square)
- Ecru felted wool for tongues (8" x 36" or 10" x 24" or 6" x 44")
- Green felted wool for pennies (1$\frac{1}{2}$" x 20" or 6" square)
- 1 skein each of *DMC* size 8 Perle cotton (Light Gray #415, variegated Green #94, Ecru) or embroidery floss
- 20 assorted $\frac{5}{8}$" Blue buttons
- Plastic coated freezer paper

INSTRUCTIONS:

1. On a 12" square of felted Ecru wool, draw a 9" circle using the given pattern.

2. Prepare appliques: Draw shapes on freezer paper and cut out on drawn line. Press shiny side of freezer paper onto wool. Cut out 9 Blue flowers.

3. Arrange flowers in a circle as shown in photo. Pin in place.

4. Blanket stitch the outer edges of the flowers, detailing with a Stem stitch or Backstitch. Make French Knots at the end of the stamens.

5. Trace tongue pattern and transfer to Ecru wool. Cut out 20. Blanket stitch around the edge with Green pearl cotton. Cut 20 Green pennies. Blanket stitch to the tongue with Green Perle cotton. Add a button with Green pearl cotton.

6. Place 5 tongues on each side of the appliqued square. Blanket stitch tongues to the back $\frac{1}{2}$" in from the edge.

7. Turn under $\frac{1}{2}$" hems all around the backing fabric. Blind stitch to the back of the rug.

Fold

CIRCLE PATTERN

On an 11" square of felted Ecru wool draw a 9" circle in center.

TONGUE PATTERN

PENNY PATTERN

Pattern for Morning Glories on page 39.

1. Add the long borders.

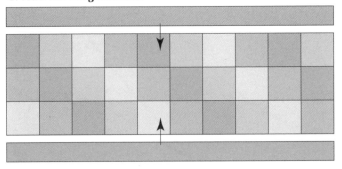

2. Add the short borders.

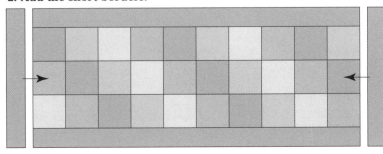

3. Stitch appliques in place.

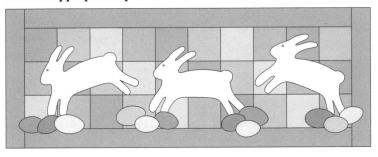

4. Add binding.

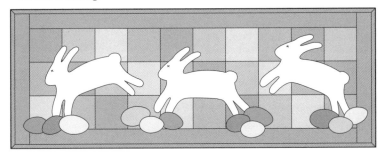

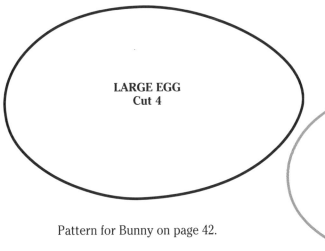

LARGE EGG
Cut 4

SMALL EGG
Cut 8

Pattern for Bunny on page 42.

Photo on page 9

Bunny Hop Table Runner
by Betsy Chutchian

Finished size: $14^1/_2$" x 39"

MATERIALS:
- Background: $^1/_8$ yd each of 5 different Green fabrics (Six 4" squares from each)
- Border: $^1/_4$ yd Sage Green marble fabric or tone on tone
- Binding: $^1/_4$ yd Green check
- Backing: $^1/_2$ yd Green check (18" x 45")
- Batting: $^1/_2$ yd (18" x 45")
- White felted wool $^1/_4$ yd (16" x 24")
- 12 assorted pastel felted wool pieces (3" x 4") each
- *DMC* size 8 Ecru Perle cotton or 3 strands embroidery floss
- *DMC* Pink embroidery floss for bunny eyes
- *DMC* size 8 pastel Perle cotton to coordinate with egg appliques
- Plastic coated freezer paper

INSTRUCTIONS:

1. Use $^1/_4$" seams to piece background Green fabrics in 3 rows of 10. Press seams in opposite directions on alternating rows. Sew the rows together. Press.

2. Cut 2 long borders $2^1/_2$" x $35^1/_2$". Add borders. Press the seam toward the border.

Cut 2 short borders $2^1/_2$" x $14^1/_2$". Add borders. Press the seam toward the border.

3. Trace patterns onto freezer paper. Press shiny side of freezer paper to wool and cut out 3 large bunnies, 8 small eggs, and 4 large eggs. Blanket stitch using Perle cotton or 3 strands of floss, or machine applique shapes to top. Stitch a Pink "x" for bunny eyes.

4. Layer the backing, batting, and top. Baste the layers together.

5. Quilting: Quilt in diagonal lines across squares but not through wool shapes. Quilting may be done before you applique if you choose.

6. Sew three $2^1/_2$" x 45" binding strips together end to end. Fold and press. Sew the binding to quilt using a $^1/_4$" seam, mitering the corners. Fold the binding over to back and sew down by hand.

Bunny Hop

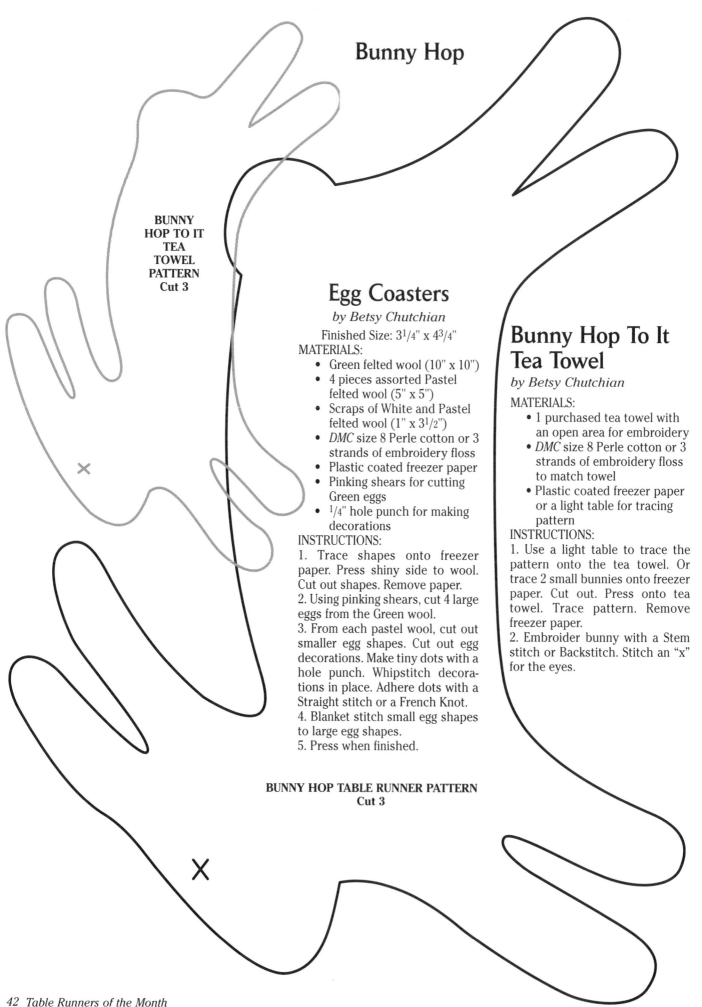

BUNNY HOP TO IT TEA TOWEL PATTERN
Cut 3

Egg Coasters
by Betsy Chutchian

Finished Size: $3^1/4$" x $4^3/4$"

MATERIALS:
- Green felted wool (10" x 10")
- 4 pieces assorted Pastel felted wool (5" x 5")
- Scraps of White and Pastel felted wool (1" x $3^1/2$")
- *DMC* size 8 Perle cotton or 3 strands of embroidery floss
- Plastic coated freezer paper
- Pinking shears for cutting Green eggs
- $1/4$" hole punch for making decorations

INSTRUCTIONS:
1. Trace shapes onto freezer paper. Press shiny side to wool. Cut out shapes. Remove paper.
2. Using pinking shears, cut 4 large eggs from the Green wool.
3. From each pastel wool, cut out smaller egg shapes. Cut out egg decorations. Make tiny dots with a hole punch. Whipstitch decorations in place. Adhere dots with a Straight stitch or a French Knot.
4. Blanket stitch small egg shapes to large egg shapes.
5. Press when finished.

BUNNY HOP TABLE RUNNER PATTERN
Cut 3

Bunny Hop To It Tea Towel
by Betsy Chutchian

MATERIALS:
- 1 purchased tea towel with an open area for embroidery
- *DMC* size 8 Perle cotton or 3 strands of embroidery floss to match towel
- Plastic coated freezer paper or a light table for tracing pattern

INSTRUCTIONS:
1. Use a light table to trace the pattern onto the tea towel. Or trace 2 small bunnies onto freezer paper. Cut out. Press onto tea towel. Trace pattern. Remove freezer paper.
2. Embroider bunny with a Stem stitch or Backstitch. Stitch an "x" for the eyes.

Bunny Hop
Egg Coasters

Posies in Baskets Table Runner

by Judith Lester

Finished size: 12$\frac{1}{2}$" x 32$\frac{1}{2}$"

MATERIALS:
- Background: $\frac{1}{8}$ yd of 3 different Pink fabrics (Eight 4$\frac{1}{2}$" squares from each)
- Binding: $\frac{1}{4}$ yd Rose print (3 cuts across width of fabric, 2$\frac{1}{2}$" x 44")
- Backing: $\frac{1}{2}$ yd Ecru and Rose stripe (15" x 40")
- Batting: $\frac{1}{2}$ yd (16" x 36")
- Blue bow fabric (8" x 10")
- Coordinating print for basket (9" x 22")
- Fabric print or felted wool for flowers: Yellow, Blue, Rose (5$\frac{1}{2}$" x 5$\frac{1}{2}$")
- Green print or felted wool for leaves: (7" x 7")
- *DMC* size 8 Perle cotton or 2-3 strands embroidery floss
- Fusible web for applique pieces

INSTRUCTIONS:

1. Use $\frac{1}{4}$" seams to piece background Pink fabrics in 3 rows of 8. Press seams in opposite directions on alternating rows. Sew the rows together. Press.

2. Trace patterns onto fusible web. Following manufacturer's directions, fuse and cut out shapes. It is recommended that you fuse and stitch one item at a time. Blanket stitch using Perle cotton or 2-3 strands of floss, or machine applique shapes to top.

3. Layer the backing, batting, and top. Baste layers together.

4. Quilting: Quilt in diagonal lines across squares but not through shapes.
Quilting can be done before doing the applique, if desired.

5. Sew the binding strips together end to end. Fold and press. Sew binding to quilt using a $\frac{1}{4}$" seam. Fold the binding over and sew down by hand.

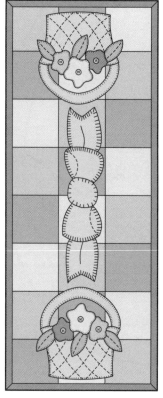

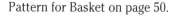

Add binding to quilt.

Pattern for Basket on page 50.

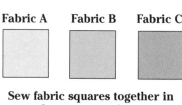

Fabric A **Fabric B** **Fabric C**

Sew fabric squares together in the sequence show.

A	B	C	A	B	C	A	B
C	A	B	C	A	B	C	A
B	C	A	B	C	A	B	C

Stitches Used for Bow and Baskets

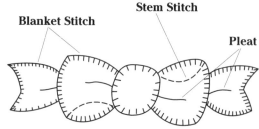

Stem Stitch

Blanket Stitch

Pleat

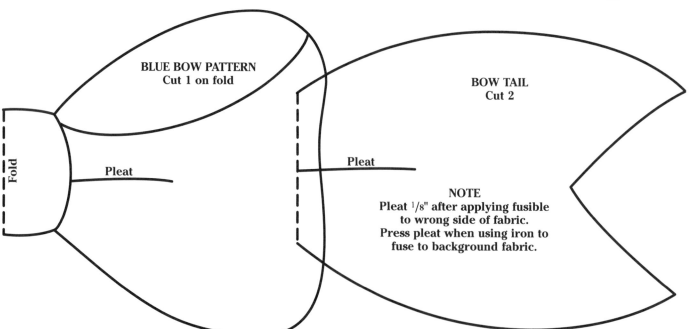

BLUE BOW PATTERN
Cut 1 on fold

BOW TAIL
Cut 2

Fold

Pleat

Pleat

NOTE
Pleat $\frac{1}{8}$" after applying fusible to wrong side of fabric. Press pleat when using iron to fuse to background fabric.

Cozy Posy Tea Cozy

by Judith Lester

Finished Size: 10" x 12¹/₂""

MATERIALS:
- Pink and Green felted wool (3¹/₂" square)
- Blue and Yellow felted wool (2¹/₂" square)
- Pink gingham fabric for outside (18" x 22")
- Green print fabric for inside (18" x 22")
- Green print or coordinating fabric for bias binding (18" x 22")
- Batting (18" square)
- *DMC* size 8 Perle cotton or embroidery floss to match wool
- Plastic coated freezer paper

INSTRUCTIONS:

1. Place batting between outside fabric and lining fabric. Machine quilt.

2. Trace cozy pattern onto freezer paper.

3. Press shiny side of freezer paper onto quilted square.

4. Cut out front and back pieces, adding ¹/₂" seam allowance.

5. Cut binding into 2¹/₄" wide bias strips. Join strips together to make one strip for the curve and one strip for bottom of cozy. Fold bias strips in half and press.

6. Trace shapes onto freezer paper, press onto wool. Cut out shapes.

7. Center shapes on outside of cozy and Blanket stitch in place.

8. Place two sides of cozy together, right sides out. Sew a generous ¹/₄" seam along curve, leaving bottom open.

9. Machine sew binding to one side of curve. Fold binding over curved edge and attach by hand to the other side.

10. Sew binding to bottom edge of cozy using the same technique.

POSY TEA COZY PATTERN

Cozy Posy Slippers

by Judith Lester

MATERIALS:
- 1 pair of purchased terry cloth Blue slippers
- Pink felted wool (3" x 6")
- Yellow felted wool (2" square)
- Plastic coated freezer paper
- *DMC* Pink and Yellow size 8 Perle cotton
- *Bohin* size 7 sharps needle
- Water soluble glue stick

INSTRUCTIONS:

1. Draw posy pattern on freezer paper. Use a nickel as a pattern for the Yellow center. Iron patterns onto wool. Cut out. Peel off paper.

2. Baste posy to slipper with glue stick. Blanket stitch with Perle cotton to secure. Use French knots to make Yellow Posy center.

3. Whipstitch around opening of slipper with Pink Perle cotton. Hide the knot under the edge of the slipper opening.

Cozy Posy Bolster

by Judith Lester

Finished Size: 23" x 42"

MATERIALS:
- ³/₄ yd of 2 coordinating prints for pillowcase
- Scraps of felted wool for posies (3¹/₂" x 9")
- Yellow felted wool for posy center (2" square)
- Green felted wool for stems and leaves (5" x 7")
- *DMC* size 8 pearl cotton or 2-3 strands of embroidery floss
- Plastic coated freezer paper
- *Bohin* Sharps size 7 needle
- 8 Pink ¹/₂" buttons
- 2 pieces coordinating *Offray* ¹/₄" wide Ecru satin ribbon 28" long
- Batting 36" x 96"

INSTRUCTIONS:

1. Remove selvages from pillowcase fabric. Cut each to 23¹/₂" x 42¹/₂".

2. On the outer pillowcase, find the center.
   Draw a gentle curve for the vine.
   Arrange wool vine and couch in place with Perle cotton.
   Arrange posies and leaves. Blanket stitch in place.
   Add posy centers with Straight stitches and French knots.

3. With right sides together, sew pillowcase pieces with a ¹/₄" seam,

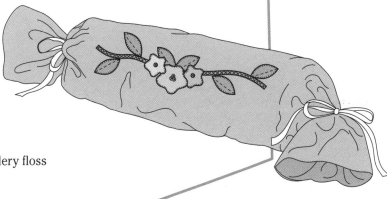

leaving an opening for turning. Turn right side out. Press. Stitch opening shut.

4. Fold batting into thirds so a 33" long pillow form is made.

5. Wrap pillowcase around batting, overlapping the long sides. Whipstitch long sides closed. Add buttons with Perle cotton.

6. Gather ends and tie with a ribbon.

Patterns for Posy Flowers on page 46.

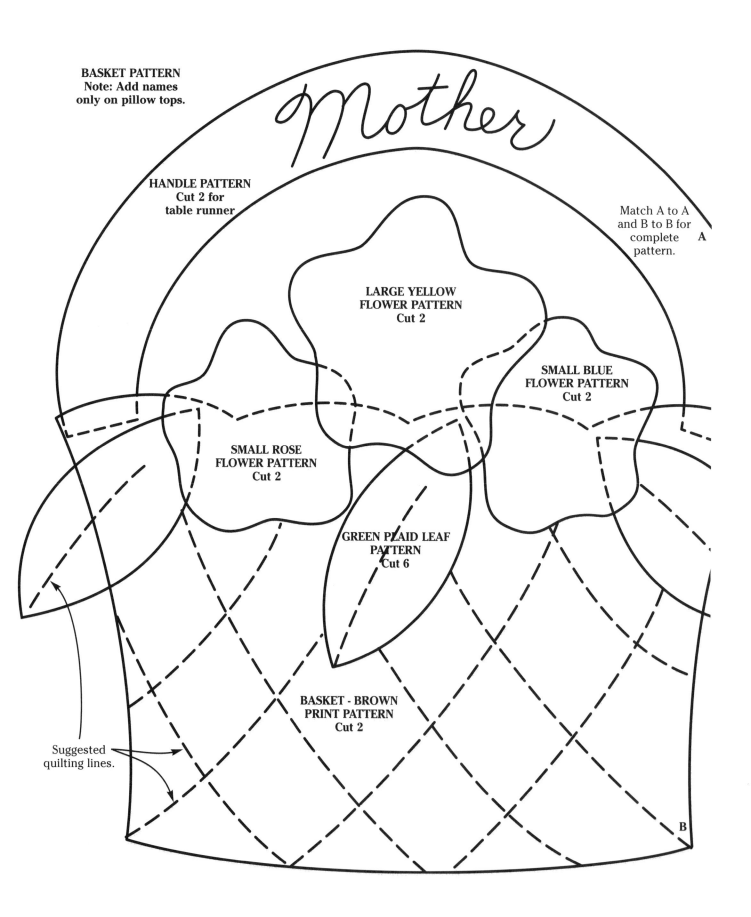

BASKET PATTERN
Note: Add names
only on pillow tops.

Mother

HANDLE PATTERN
Cut 2 for
table runner

Match A to A
and B to B for
complete
pattern. **A**

**LARGE YELLOW
FLOWER PATTERN**
Cut 2

**SMALL BLUE
FLOWER PATTERN**
Cut 2

**SMALL ROSE
FLOWER PATTERN**
Cut 2

**GREEN PLAID LEAF
PATTERN**
Cut 6

**BASKET - BROWN
PRINT PATTERN**
Cut 2

Suggested
quilting lines.

B

Posies

Photo on page 13

A

B

Pink Posies for Mother Pillow Top

by Judith Lester

Finished Size: 21" square, fits a 14" pillow form

MATERIALS:
- White on Ecru print for embroidery square (11" x 11")
- Solid White fabric for quilt backing (11" x 11")
- Batting (11" x 11")
- *DMC* Pink size 8 Perle cotton or 2 strands of embroidery floss
- Inner Border: 2 side Rose borders ($1^1/4$" x 10"); top/bottom Rose borders ($1^1/4$" x 11")
- Outer Border: 2 side print borders (2" x $11^1/2$"); top/bottom print borders (2" x $14^1/2$")
- Inner Ruffle 4" wide x 3 $3/4$ yd long (4" x 135")
- Outer Ruffle 7" wide x 3 $3/4$ yd long (7" x 135")
- Pillow back: 2 rectangles (9" x $14^1/2$")
- 14" pillow form

INSTRUCTIONS:

1. Trace design onto Ecru square. Embroider using a Stem stitch for the basket and a Back stitch for the name.

2. Layer backing, batting, and embroidered square. Pin baste layers together. Quilt around the basket. Trim to 10" square.

3. Sew side borders to the square with a $1/4$" seam. Press toward border. Sew borders to top and bottom of square. Press toward border.

4. Ruffle: Fold each ruffle in half, raw edges together. Press. With raw edges together, use a $1/4$" seam to sew the small ruffle to the wide ruffle. Gather raw edges. Baste gathered ruffle to the right side of the pillow top.

5. Pillow back: Press $1/4$" along 1 long side of each rectangle. Fold over $1/2$" again. Press. Stitch. Overlap stitched edges so the outside cut edge matches the size of the pillow top. Baste overlapped edges together. This will later become the opening for the pillow. You may add buttons, button holes, or velcro to close this opening.

6. Layer basted ruffle between embroidered top and back. Stitch layers together using a $1/2$" seam, slightly rounding the corners.

7. Remove basting. Turn pillow top right side out. Press. Insert pillow form.

Blue Posies for Alice Pillow Top

by Judith Lester

Finished Size: 21" square fits a 14" pillow form

MATERIALS:
- White on White print for embroidery square (11" x 11")
- Solid White fabric for quilt backing (11" x 11")
- Batting (11" x 11")
- *DMC* Blue size 8 Perle cotton or 2 strands of embroidery floss
- Border: 2 side Rose borders (2" x $10^1/2$") and top/bottom Rose borders (2" x $13^1/2$")
- Inner Ruffle $2^1/2$" wide x 3 $3/4$ yd long ($2^1/4$" x 135")
- Outer Ruffle 7" wide x 3 $3/4$ yd long (7" x 135")
- Pillow back: 2 rectangles (9" x $14^1/2$")
- 14" pillow form

INSTRUCTIONS:

1. Trace design onto White square. Embroider using a Stem stitch for the basket and a Back stitch for the name.

2. Layer backing, batting, and embroidered square. Pin baste layers together. Quilt around the basket. (See diagram.) Trim to $10^1/2$" square.

3. Sew side borders to the square with a $1/4$" seam. Press toward border. Sew borders to top and bottom of square. Press toward border.

4. Ruffle: Use a $1/4$" seam to sew the two ruffle pieces together, making a string $8^3/4$" x 135". Press seam open. Fold ruffle in half. Press. Gather raw edges. Baste gathered ruffle to the right side of the pillow top.

5. Pillow back: Press $1/4$" along 1 long side of each rectangle. Fold over $1/2$" again. Press. Stitch. Overlap stitched edges so the outside cut edge matches the size of the pillow top. Baste overlapped edges together. This will later become the opening for the pillow. You may add buttons, button holes, or velcro to close this opening.

6. Layer basted ruffle between embroidered top and back. Stitch layers together using a $1/2$" seam, slightly rounding the corners.

7. Remove basting. Turn the pillow top right side out. Press. Insert pillow form.

 **June**

Photo on page 15

Strip Piecing for Table Runner

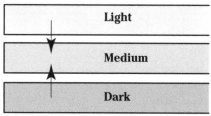

| Light |
| Medium |
| Dark |

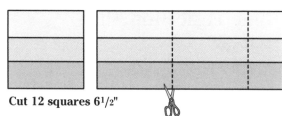

Cut 12 squares 6¹/₂"

Block Placement for Rail Fence

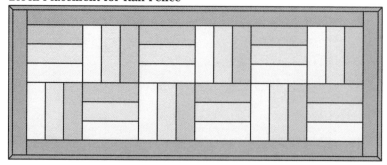

Add appliques and binding.

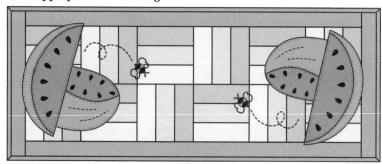

**TABLE RUNNER
BEE EMBROIDERY
PATTERN**

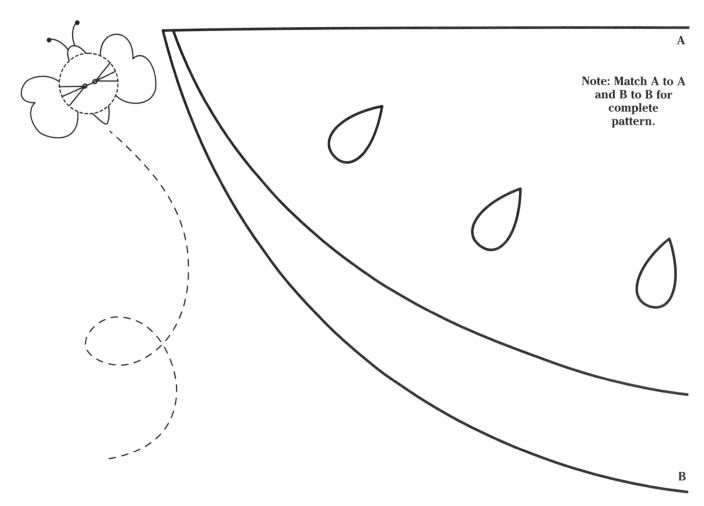

A

**Note: Match A to A
and B to B for
complete
pattern.**

B

Watermelon Table Runner

by Betty Edgell

Finished Size: 16" x 40"

MATERIALS:
- Background: $^1/4$ yd each Light Green, Medium Green, Dark Green (9" x 45")
- Border: $^1/4$ yd for 2 long borders ($2^1/4$" x $36^1/2$"), 2 short borders ($2^1/4$" x $16^1/2$")
- Binding: $^1/4$ yd makes 3 Green strips ($2^1/4$" x 45")
- Backing: $^1/2$ yd Light Green (18" x 45")
- Batting: $^1/2$ yd (18" x 42")
- Red felted wool (16" x 16")
- Green felted wool (16" x 16")
- 26 small pieces Black or Brown felted wool for seeds (6" x 6")
- *DMC* size 8 Perle cotton or embroidery floss to match wool
- *DMC* Black and Yellow size 8 Perle cotton or embroidery floss for bees
- 2 Black buttons for bee bodies
- *Bohin* size 8 sharps needles or embroidery needles
- Plastic coated freezer paper

INSTRUCTIONS:
1. Cut each Green fabric into 2 strips $2^1/2$" wide.
2. Use $^1/4$" seam allowances to sew strips in order: Light, Medium, Dark. Press to dark.
3. Cut strips into twelve $6^1/2$" squares.
4. Piece together according to the diagram.
5. Add long borders. Press toward border. Add short borders. Press toward border.
6. Layer the backing, batting and the assembled top. Center the top, right side up, on the batting. Baste all the layers together.
7. Quilt as desired with Perle cotton or 2 strands of embroidery floss. Remove the basting stitches. Trim the batting even with the edges of the quilt top.
8. Sew the binding strips together. Fold in half. Press. Bind the edges.
9. Trace patterns onto freezer paper. Press onto wool and cut out pieces. Applique with Blanket stitch and Perle cotton or embroidery floss. Stem stitch details on melon rind. Attach Black button for bee body with Gold embroidery floss. With pencil, draw bee wings and bee line, then embroider with 2 strands of Black floss (a Back stitch or Stem stitch for the wings and antennae and a Running stitch for bee line).

Pattern for Half Watermelon on page 50.

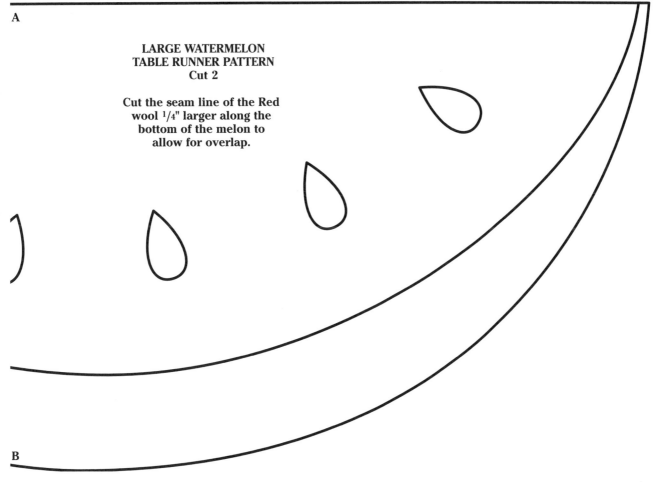

A

**LARGE WATERMELON
TABLE RUNNER PATTERN
Cut 2**

**Cut the seam line of the Red
wool $^1/4$" larger along the
bottom of the melon to
allow for overlap.**

B

June

Photo on page 15

Watermelon Table Runner

Continued from page 49.

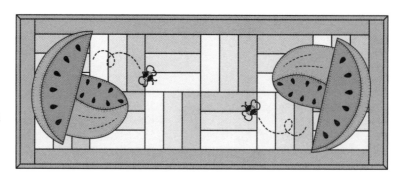

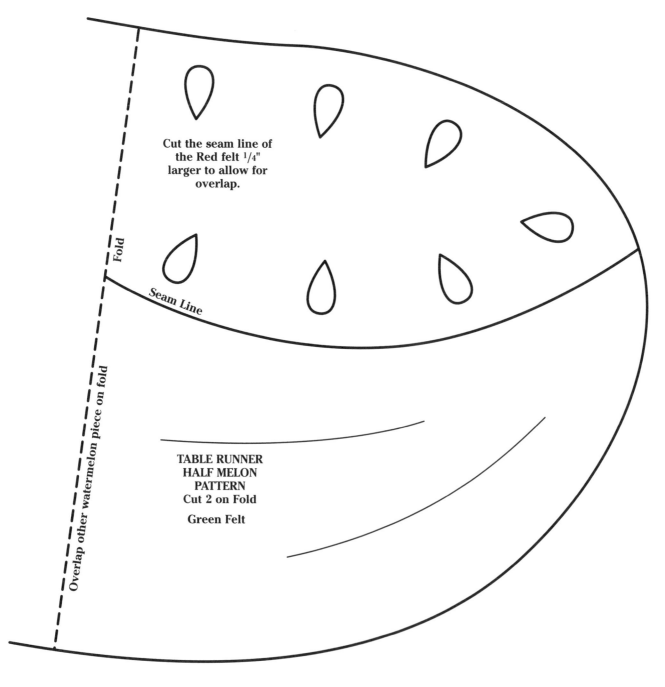

Cut the seam line of the Red felt 1/4" larger to allow for overlap.

Fold

Seam Line

Overlap other watermelon piece on fold

**TABLE RUNNER
HALF MELON
PATTERN
Cut 2 on Fold**

Green Felt

Blanket stitch around watermelon. Sew beads in place.

Blanket stitch this edge for checkbook.

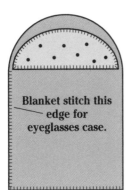

Blanket stitch this edge for eyeglasses case.

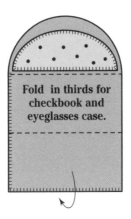

Fold in thirds for checkbook and eyeglasses case.

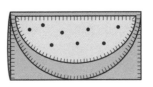

Blanket stitch closed the round edge of Green felt for eyeglasses case.

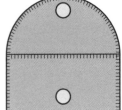

Blanket stitch sides closed for checkbook. Blanket stitch the round edge. Attach Velcro for closure.

Melon Checkbook Cover

by Betty Edgell

Finished size: $3^1/2$" x 7"

MATERIALS:
- Coat weight Green felted wool (7" x 10")
- Red felted wool (3" x $6^1/2$")
- *DMC* size 8 Perle cotton (Ecru, Red, Green) or embroidery floss to match
- 7 Black beads for seeds
- Black sewing thread, needle for sewing on beads
- Lite Steam-A-Seam 2 fusible web

INSTRUCTIONS:

1. Use the pattern to cut Green fabric.

2. Draw the watermelon pattern onto fusible web. Follow manufacturer's directions for fusing to wool. Position watermelon in place. Fuse.

3. Blanket stitch around watermelon. Sew beads in place.

4. Fold Green wool to form checkbook holder. Blanket stitch sides closed. Blanket stitch edge of cover.

Melon Eyeglasses Case

by Betty Edgell

Finished size: $3^1/2$" x 7"

MATERIALS:
- Coat weight Green felted wool (7" x 10")
- Red felted wool ($3^1/2$" x $6^1/2$")
- *DMC* size 8 Perle cotton (Ecru, Red, Green) or embroidery floss to match
- 8 Black beads for seeds
- Black sewing thread, needle for sewing on beads
- Lite Steam-A-Seam 2 fusible web

INSTRUCTIONS:

1. Use the pattern to cut Green fabric.

2. Draw the watermelon pattern onto fusible web. Follow manufacturer's directions for fusing to wool. Position watermelon in place. Fuse.

3. Blanket stitch around watermelon. Sew beads in place.

4. Fold Green wool in thirds to form case. Blanket stitch rounded edge to case, being careful not to go through all 3 layers. Blanket stitch one side closed. Blanket stitch around the opening.

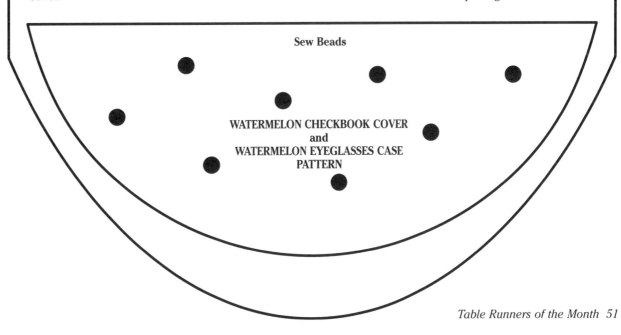

Sew Beads

WATERMELON CHECKBOOK COVER
and
WATERMELON EYEGLASSES CASE
PATTERN

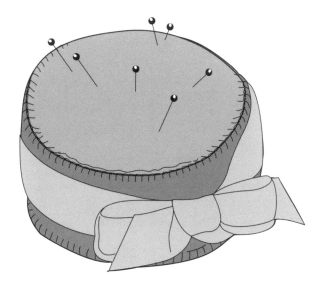

Watermelon Pincushion

by Betsy Chutchian and Betty Edgell

Finished size: 2" tall x 4³/4" diameter

MATERIALS:
- Green felted wool for sides and bottom (15" x 18")
- Red felted wool for top (5" square)
- Cardboard circle (4³/4" diameter)
- 24" of 1" wide Green and Pink *Offray* sheer ribbon
- 24" of ¹/2" wide Green *Offray* sheer ribbon
- Green wool for sides (2" x 14")
- Natural wool or cotton fiber for stuffing
- *DMC* size 8 Perle cotton (Ecru and Green) or embroidery floss to match

INSTRUCTIONS:
1. Sew side wool into a circle that fits the bottom.
2. Sew bottom to side with a Blanket stitch.
3. Insert cardboard into bottom.
4. Sew ³/4 of the top to the side and stuff. Finish sewing top.
5. Wrap with ribbon. Tack in place if desired.

**WATERMELON
PINCUSHION
CARDBOARD CIRCLE
PATTERN**

Hollyhock Tote Bag

by Judith Lester

Finished size: 12" x 18"

MATERIALS:
- Outer bag and handles: ¹/2 yd Brown print
- Lining: ¹/2 yard coordinating print
- Green felted wool for stems and leaves (8" x 10")
- Yellow felted wool for flowers (4" x 4")
- 3 Pink ⁷/8" buttons
- 9 Pink ³/4" buttons
- 2 Brown ⁷/8" buttons
- *DMC* Yellow size 8 Perle cotton or 3 strands embroidery floss
- Plastic coated freezer paper
- 1" square *Velcro*

INSTRUCTIONS:

1. Cut bag and lining fabric 14" x 44". Cut 2 handles 4" x 22" each.

2. Fold outer bag fabric 14" x 22". Mark applique placement. (See diagram.)

3. Trace pattern for leaves, stems and buds onto freezer paper. Press on wool. Cut out pieces. Cut 12 dime size or smaller Yellow circles for flower centers. Position leaves, buttons, and flower centers. Sew in place.

4. Fold handles with right sides together to 2" x 22". Sew a ¹/4" seam along the long side. Leave the ends open. Turn to the right side. Press. Quilt the handles.

5. With right sides together, sew the side seam of the bag and the lining fabric. (See diagram.)

6. Turn the bag right side out. Place the bag inside the lining. Do NOT turn lining fabric. You will see the wrong side of the lining on the outside. If you look inside, you will see the wrong side of the bag. (See diagram.) Position the handles between the lining and bag as shown in diagram.

7. Sew around the top. See diagram.

8. Open into a long tube. See diagram.

9. Sew bottom seam of the bag. Sew corners. (See diagram.)

10. Sew bottom seam of lining, leaving a 6" opening in the center for turning. Sew lining corners.

11. Turn right side out. Stitch opening closed. Stuff lining into bag.

12. Topstitch the top of the bag.

13. Sew velcro to top center inside bag. Add buttons outside.

> "Pressing is not an option."
> Betty Edgell

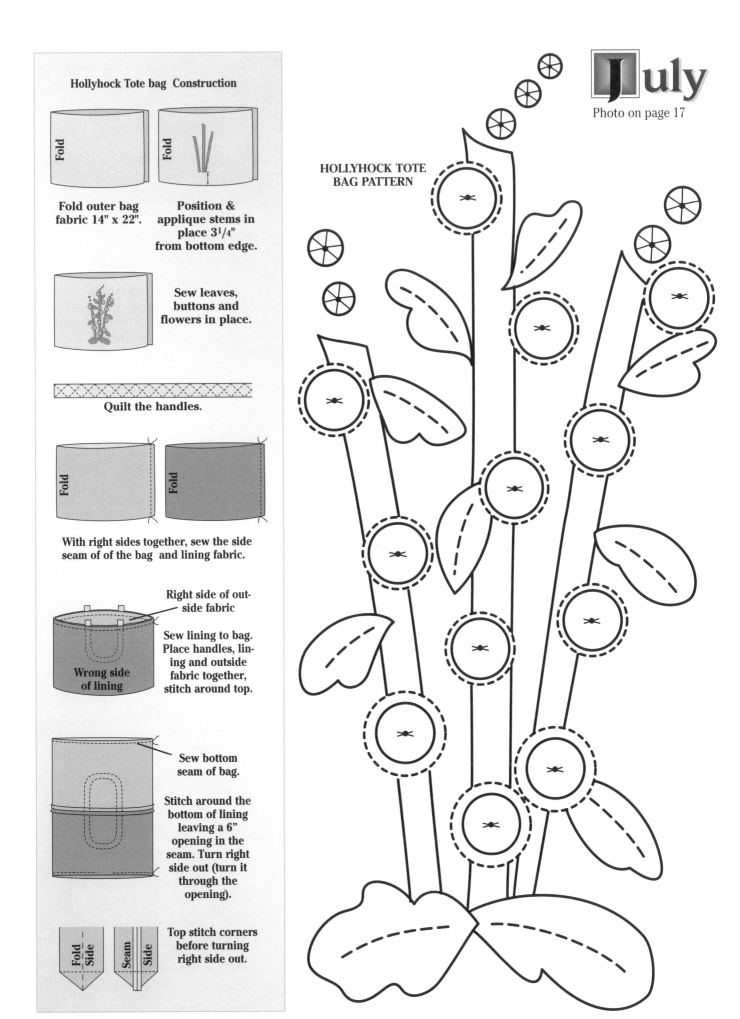

Hollyhock Tote bag Construction

Fold outer bag fabric 14" x 22".

Position & applique stems in place 3¹/4" from bottom edge.

Sew leaves, buttons and flowers in place.

Quilt the handles.

With right sides together, sew the side seam of of the bag and lining fabric.

Right side of outside fabric

Wrong side of lining

Sew lining to bag. Place handles, lining and outside fabric together, stitch around top.

Sew bottom seam of bag.

Stitch around the bottom of lining leaving a 6" opening in the seam. Turn right side out (turn it through the opening).

Top stitch corners before turning right side out.

Photo on page 17

July

HOLLYHOCK TOTE BAG PATTERN

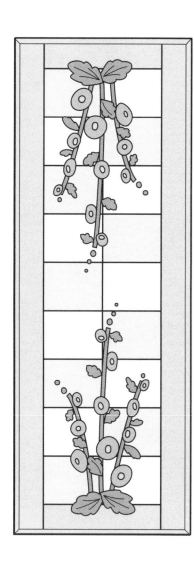

Hollyhock Table Runner

by Judith Lester

Finished size: $14^1/2$" x $40^1/2$"

MATERIALS:
- Background: $1/6$ yd each of 2 shades of White with Blue print (6" x 45")
- Border: $1/4$ yard medium Blue print (9" x 45")
- Binding: $1/4$ yard same as border or coordinating fabric (9" x 45")
- Backing: 18" x 45"
- Batting: 18" x 45"
- Green fabric for stems cut on bias (10" x 10")
- Pink felted wool for flowers (7" x 16")
- Green felted wool for leaves and buds (7" x 16")
- Yellow felted wool for flower center (2" x 5")
- *DMC* size 8 Pink, Green, and Yellow Perle cotton
- Plastic coated freezer paper

INSTRUCTIONS:

1. Cut 9 White with Blue rectangles from each fabric $4^1/2$" x $5^1/2$", 2 short borders ($2^1/2$" x $10^1/2$"), 2 long borders ($2^1/2$" x 41"). Cut 3 strips of binding $2^1/2$" by width of fabric.

2. Alternate the White and Blue rectangles 9 across, 2 down. (See diagram.) Use $1/4$" seams to sew the rectangles together. Press the seams in different directions on alternate rows. Sew the rows together.

3. Add the short borders. Press the seam toward the border. Add the long borders. Press the seam toward the border.

4. Stems: Cut 3 bias strips from stem fabric $1^1/2$" wide. Cut left stem $1^1/2$" x 8". Cut the middle stem $1^1/2$" x 13". Cut the right stem $1^1/2$" x 10". Fold wrong sides together and stitch $1/8$" seam. Press. Arrange stems on each end of the background. Applique in place.

5. Flowers & Leaves: Trace the patterns onto freezer paper and cut out. Press on wool. Cut out flower and leaf pieces. Position and applique the flowers and leaves, using Perle cotton or embroidery thread.

6. Baste layers together. Hand or machine quilt as desired.

7. Sew the binding strips together. Fold and press. Sew binding to quilt using a $1/4$" seam. Fold the binding over and sew down by hand.

Note: Left stem is #1, center stem is #2, and right stem is #3. Flower and leaf patterns are labeled alphabetically from bottom to top for each stem number.

HOLLYHOCK TABLE RUNNER PATTERNS

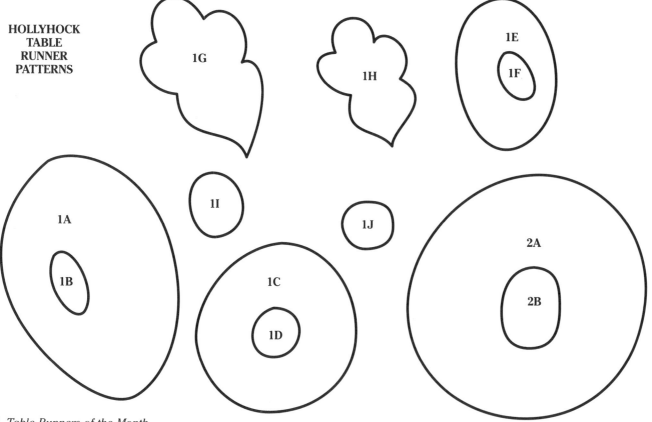

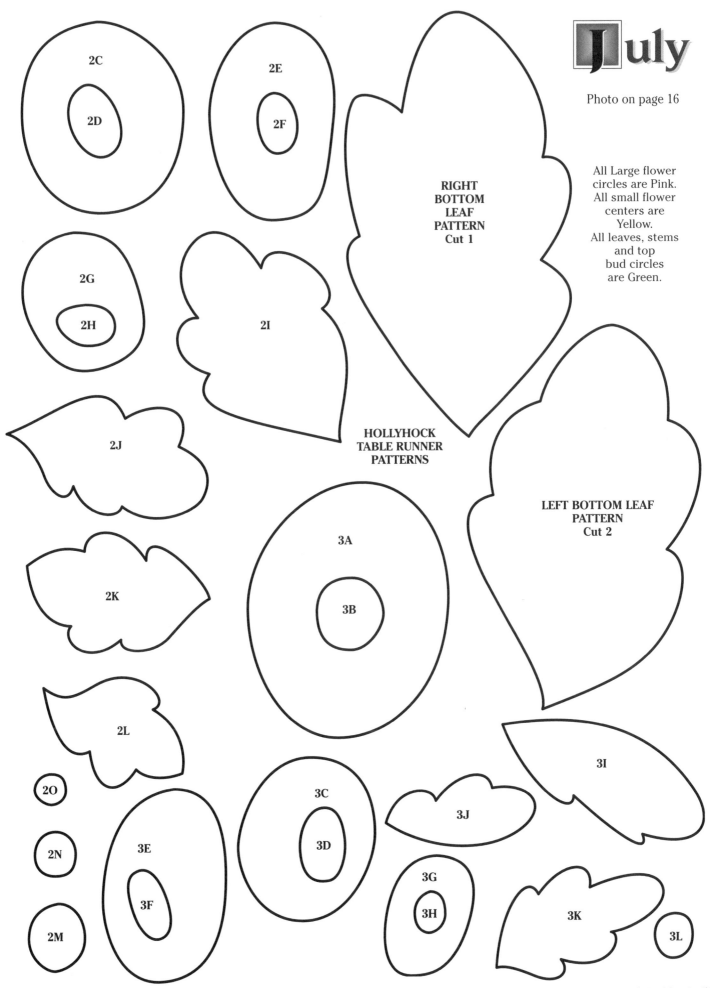

July

Photo on page 16

All Large flower circles are Pink. All small flower centers are Yellow. All leaves, stems and top bud circles are Green.

2C

2D

2E

2F

RIGHT BOTTOM LEAF PATTERN Cut 1

2G

2H

2I

2J

HOLLYHOCK TABLE RUNNER PATTERNS

LEFT BOTTOM LEAF PATTERN Cut 2

2K

3A

3B

2L

3I

2O

3C

3D

3J

2N

3E

3F

3G

3H

3K

2M

3L

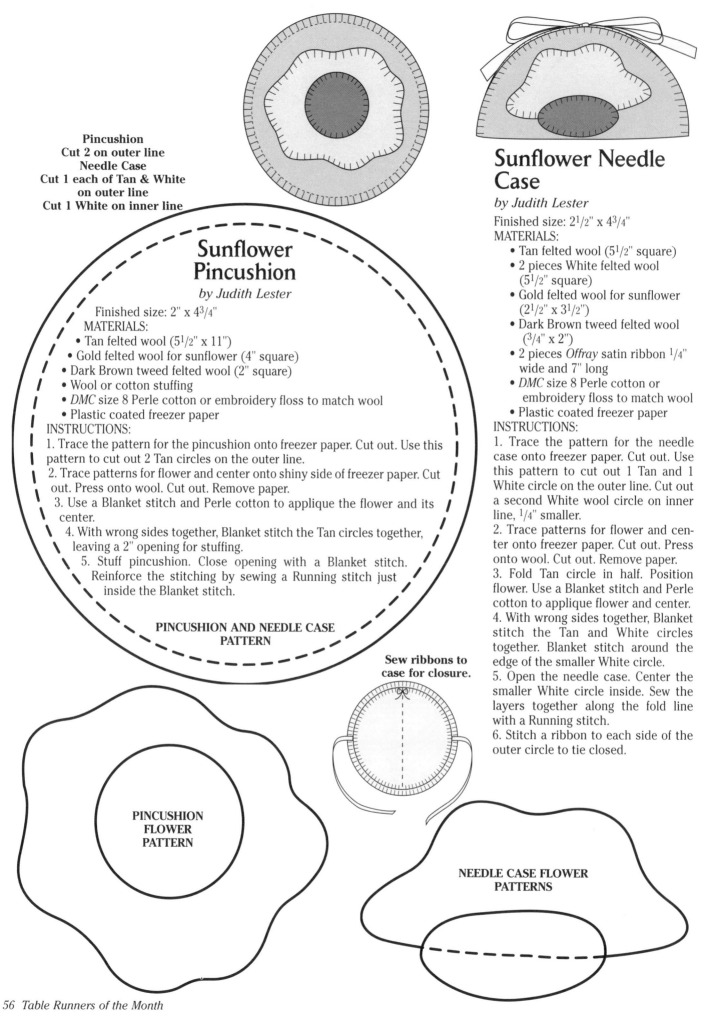

Pincushion
Cut 2 on outer line
Needle Case
Cut 1 each of Tan & White
on outer line
Cut 1 White on inner line

Sunflower Pincushion

by Judith Lester

Finished size: 2" x 4³/4"
MATERIALS:
- Tan felted wool (5¹/2" x 11")
- Gold felted wool for sunflower (4" square)
- Dark Brown tweed felted wool (2" square)
- Wool or cotton stuffing
- *DMC* size 8 Perle cotton or embroidery floss to match wool
- Plastic coated freezer paper

INSTRUCTIONS:
1. Trace the pattern for the pincushion onto freezer paper. Cut out. Use this pattern to cut out 2 Tan circles on the outer line.
2. Trace patterns for flower and center onto shiny side of freezer paper. Cut out. Press onto wool. Cut out. Remove paper.
3. Use a Blanket stitch and Perle cotton to applique the flower and its center.
4. With wrong sides together, Blanket stitch the Tan circles together, leaving a 2" opening for stuffing.
5. Stuff pincushion. Close opening with a Blanket stitch. Reinforce the stitching by sewing a Running stitch just inside the Blanket stitch.

PINCUSHION AND NEEDLE CASE PATTERN

PINCUSHION FLOWER PATTERN

Sew ribbons to case for closure.

Sunflower Needle Case

by Judith Lester

Finished size: 2¹/2" x 4³/4"
MATERIALS:
- Tan felted wool (5¹/2" square)
- 2 pieces White felted wool (5¹/2" square)
- Gold felted wool for sunflower (2¹/2" x 3¹/2")
- Dark Brown tweed felted wool (³/4" x 2")
- 2 pieces *Offray* satin ribbon ¹/4" wide and 7" long
- *DMC* size 8 Perle cotton or embroidery floss to match wool
- Plastic coated freezer paper

INSTRUCTIONS:
1. Trace the pattern for the needle case onto freezer paper. Cut out. Use this pattern to cut out 1 Tan and 1 White circle on the outer line. Cut out a second White wool circle on inner line, ¹/4" smaller.
2. Trace patterns for flower and center onto freezer paper. Cut out. Press onto wool. Cut out. Remove paper.
3. Fold Tan circle in half. Position flower. Use a Blanket stitch and Perle cotton to applique flower and center.
4. With wrong sides together, Blanket stitch the Tan and White circles together. Blanket stitch around the edge of the smaller White circle.
5. Open the needle case. Center the smaller White circle inside. Sew the layers together along the fold line with a Running stitch.
6. Stitch a ribbon to each side of the outer circle to tie closed.

NEEDLE CASE FLOWER PATTERNS

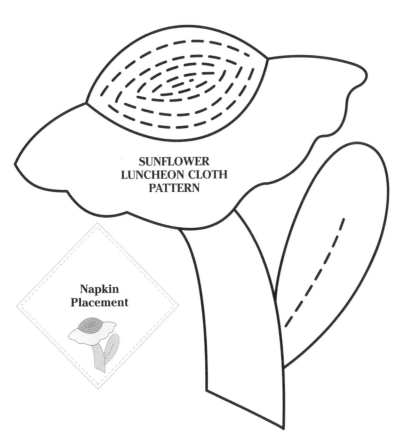

SUNFLOWER
LUNCHEON CLOTH
PATTERN

Napkin
Placement

Sunflower Luncheon Cloth Placement

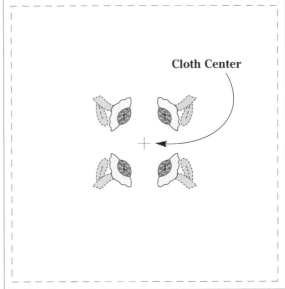

Cloth Center

Sunflower Luncheon Cloth and Napkins

by Judith Lester

Finished size: Tablecloth: 42" square
Napkins: 10" square
MATERIALS:
- 1¹/₂ yards White or Ecru fabric
- Yellow, Green, and Brown fabric crayons or paint
- *DMC* size 8 Perle cotton or embroidery floss to match crayons or paint

INSTRUCTIONS:
1. Cut a 44" square for the tablecloth. Hem to 42". Sew a Running stitch by hand around the hem of the table-cloth with Green floss if desired. Cut 4 napkins 11" square. Hem to 10". Prewash and press fabric. Do not starch or use sizing when pressing. If you hem first, it prevents raveling.
2. Trace the flower pattern onto the napkins and tablecloth.
3. Follow the manufacturer's direc-tions to color or paint and heat set the designs.
4. Embroider a Stem stitch around the Yellow and Brown parts of the flower. Use Running stitches inside the Brown part of the flower and for the stem and leaves.

Sunflowers in a Rusty Bucket Table Runner

by Judith Lester

Photo on page 18

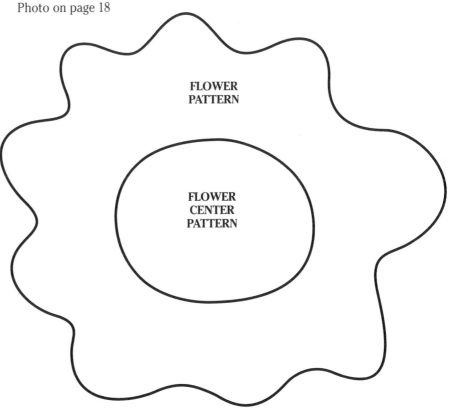

FLOWER
PATTERN

FLOWER
CENTER
PATTERN

Bucket Table Runner continued on page 59.

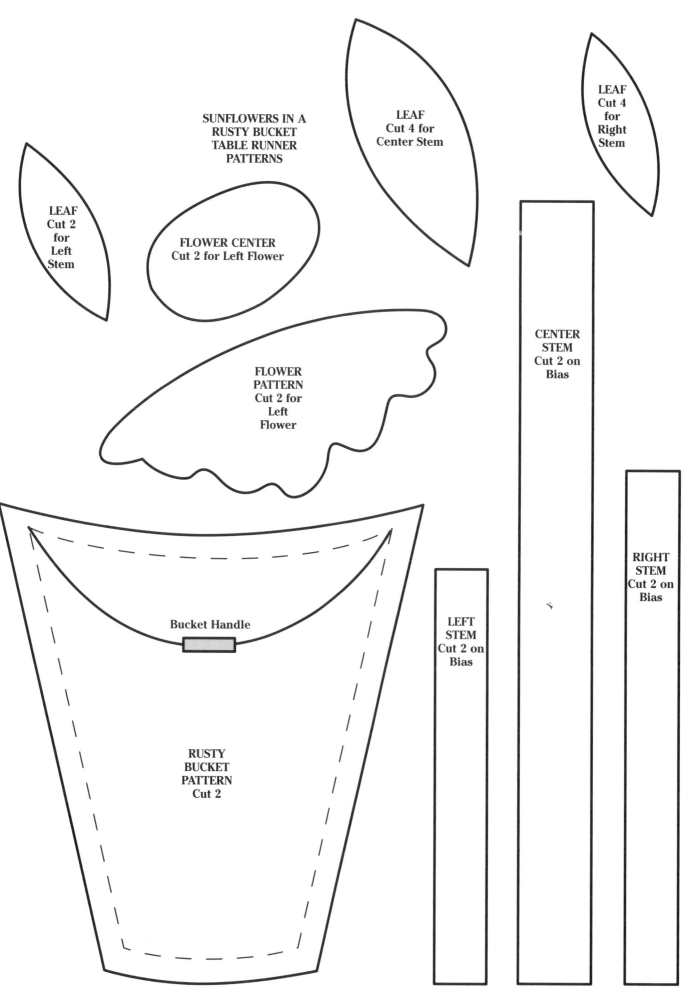

SUNFLOWERS IN A
RUSTY BUCKET
TABLE RUNNER
PATTERNS

LEAF
Cut 2
for
Left
Stem

FLOWER CENTER
Cut 2 for Left Flower

LEAF
Cut 4 for
Center Stem

LEAF
Cut 4
for
Right
Stem

CENTER
STEM
Cut 2 on
Bias

FLOWER
PATTERN
Cut 2 for
Left
Flower

RIGHT
STEM
Cut 2 on
Bias

Bucket Handle

LEFT
STEM
Cut 2 on
Bias

RUSTY
BUCKET
PATTERN
Cut 2

Sunflowers in a Rusty Bucket Table Runner

by Judith Lester

Finished size: $14^1/4$" x $40^1/2$"

MATERIALS:
- Background: Cream with Brown checkerboard ($10^1/2$" x $36^1/2$")
- Border: $1/2$ yard medium Brown print ($14^1/4$" x $40^1/2$")
- Binding: fat $1/4$ yard dark Brown check (18" x 22")
- Backing: $1/2$ yard medium Brown print (18" x 45")
- Batting: 18" x 45"
- 2 pieces of bucket fabric (6" square)
- Green felted wool for stems and leaves (8" square)
- Brown tweed felted wool for flower centers (4" x 5")
- Yellow felted wool for flowers (6" x 14")
- *DMC* size 8 Ecru, Brown, Green, and Yellow Perle cotton
- Plastic coated freezer paper

INSTRUCTIONS:

1. Trace the pattern for the curved ends of the background onto freezer paper. Fold the Cream background in half so it is $10^1/2$" x 18". Position the freezer paper on the ends and press in place. For greater accuracy, fold fabric and cut both ends at the same time. Press a $1/4$" seam all the way around. Clip curves if needed.

2. Center the Cream background on the medium Brown border. Baste in place. Draw a line $2^1/4$" from the curved edge of the Cream. Cut out the curve on the border print.

3. Blanket stitch the Cream background to the medium Brown. Turn fabric over and cut away the Brown fabric behind the Cream.

4. Trace patterns for applique onto freezer paper. Cut out. Press onto fabric and wool. Cut out. Press under a $1/4$" hem around buckets. Pin pieces in place or follow manufacturer's instructions to fuse with Steam-A-Seam. Blanket stitch appliques. Stem stitch the bucket handle. Add a Satin stitch to the bucket handle if desired. Flower centers are Satin stitched with a sewing machine in the sample, then Blanket stitched by hand.

5. Baste layers together. Hand or machine quilt as desired.

6. Fold the binding fat quarter on the diagonal. Press. Cut on the fold. Place triangles together. Cut strips $2^1/2$" wide. Sew the binding strips together to make a strip 100" long. Fold binding with wrong sides together and press so you have a piece $1^1/4$" x 100". Sew binding to quilt using a $1/4$" seam, taking care not to stretch the binding. Fold the binding over and sew down by hand or machine.

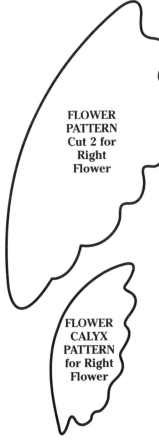

FLOWER PATTERN
Cut 2 for Right Flower

FLOWER CALYX PATTERN for Right Flower

TABLE RUNNER CURVE PATTERN
Cut 1

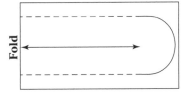

Fold

For greater accuracy, cut both ends at the same time.

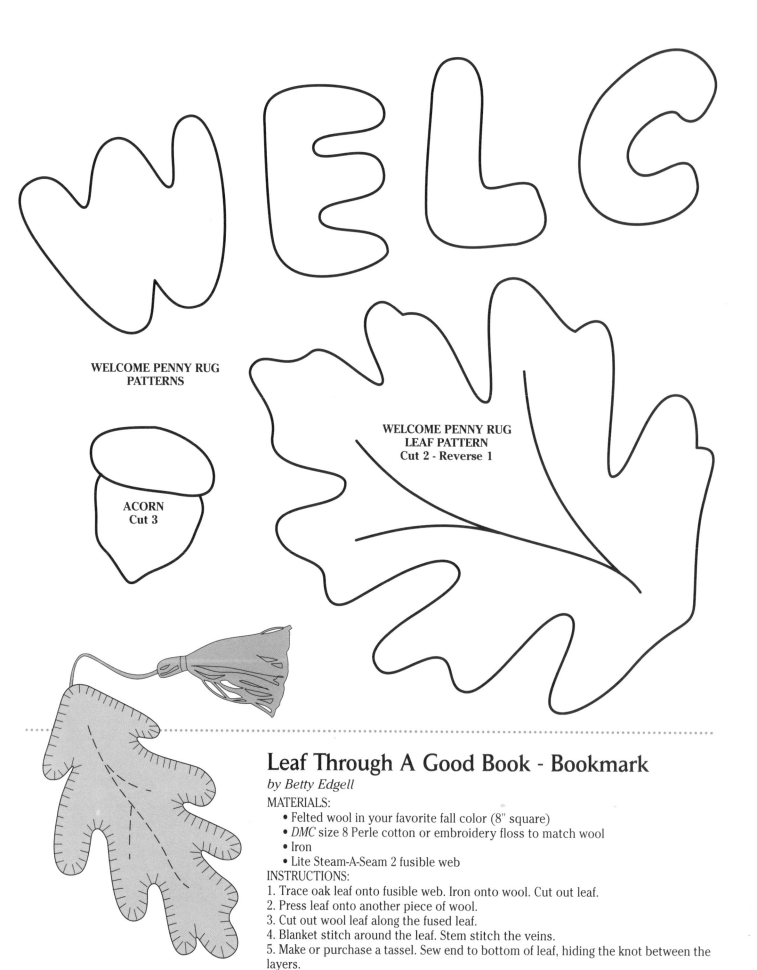

WELCOME PENNY RUG PATTERNS

ACORN Cut 3

WELCOME PENNY RUG LEAF PATTERN Cut 2 - Reverse 1

Leaf Through A Good Book - Bookmark

by Betty Edgell

MATERIALS:
- Felted wool in your favorite fall color (8" square)
- *DMC* size 8 Perle cotton or embroidery floss to match wool
- Iron
- Lite Steam-A-Seam 2 fusible web

INSTRUCTIONS:
1. Trace oak leaf onto fusible web. Iron onto wool. Cut out leaf.
2. Press leaf onto another piece of wool.
3. Cut out wool leaf along the fused leaf.
4. Blanket stitch around the leaf. Stem stitch the veins.
5. Make or purchase a tassel. Sew end to bottom of leaf, hiding the knot between the layers.

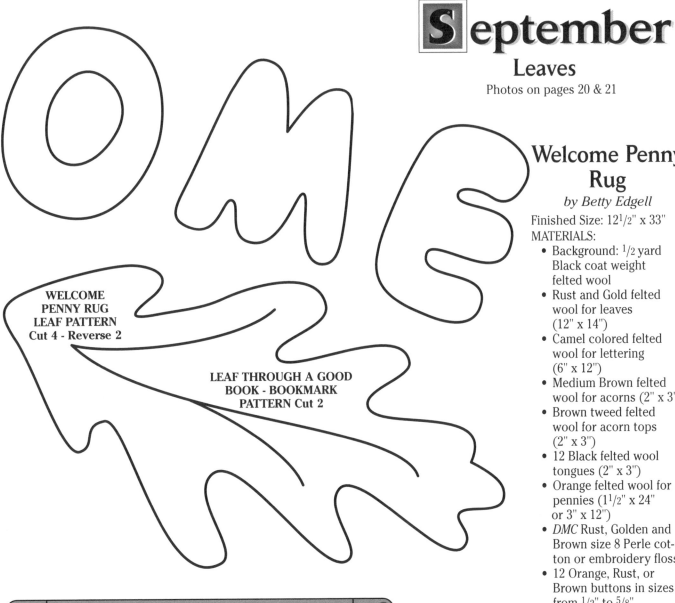

**WELCOME
PENNY RUG
LEAF PATTERN
Cut 4 - Reverse 2**

**LEAF THROUGH A GOOD
BOOK - BOOKMARK
PATTERN Cut 2**

Welcome Penny Rug
by Betty Edgell

Finished Size: 12$1/2$" x 33"
MATERIALS:
- Background: $1/2$ yard Black coat weight felted wool
- Rust and Gold felted wool for leaves (12" x 14")
- Camel colored felted wool for lettering (6" x 12")
- Medium Brown felted wool for acorns (2" x 3")
- Brown tweed felted wool for acorn tops (2" x 3")
- 12 Black felted wool tongues (2" x 3")
- Orange felted wool for pennies (1$1/2$" x 24" or 3" x 12")
- *DMC* Rust, Golden and Brown size 8 Perle cotton or embroidery floss
- 12 Orange, Rust, or Brown buttons in sizes from $1/2$" to $5/8$"
- Lite Steam-A-Seam 2 fusible web
- Black sewing thread

INSTRUCTIONS:
1. Cut Penny Rug background 12$1/2$" x 28".
2. Prepare appliques: Draw shapes on fusible web and cut out on drawn line. Cut out 4 small leaves and 2 large leaves.
3. Trace lettering and acorn pieces onto fusible web, following manufacturer's instructions.
4. Arrange applique pieces. Blanket stitch the outer edges of all pieces, detailing leaves with a Stem stitch or Backstitch.
5. Blanket stitch around the rug with Rust pearl cotton.
6. Trace tongue pattern on freezer paper. Cut out on line. Press to Black wool. Cut out 12. Blanket stitch around edge with Rust Perle cotton. Cut 12 Orange pennies. Blanket stitch to tongue with Golden Perle cotton. Add a button with Golden Perle cotton.
7. Place 6 tongues on each end of rug. Sew tongues to the back, $1/2$" in from the edge, with Black thread.

**PENNY RUG
ORANGE
PENNIES
PATTERN
Cut 12**

**PENNY RUG TONGUE
PATTERN
Cut 12**

Photo on page 20

Table Runner Block Layout

Add Long Borders

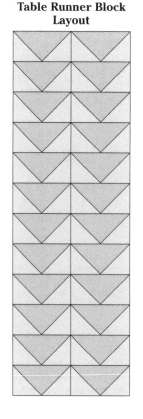

Geese Cutting Diagram

Sky Cutting Diagram

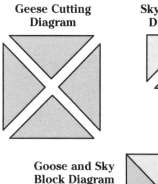

Goose and Sky Block Diagram

Add short borders and appliques

Add binding

Patterns for Leaves on pages 60 & 61.

Flying South Table Runner

by Betty Edgell

Finished Size: 15^1/$_2$" x 39^1/$_2$"

MATERIALS:
- Background: 2 hand-dyed fabrics for geese (18" x 22")
- 2 Blue hand-dyed fabrics for sky (18" x 22")
- Border: ^{1}/$_2$ yd Brown marbled fabric (18" x 45")
- Binding: ^{1}/$_4$ yd makes 3 Brown strips (2^1/$_4$" x 45")
- Backing: ^{1}/$_2$ yd Blue hand-dyed (18" x 45")
- Batting: 18" x 42"
- 7 pieces Leaf colored felted wool 5" x 6"
- *DMC* size 8 Perle cotton to match leaf wool
- Plastic coated freezer paper

INSTRUCTIONS:

1. Cut each goose fabric into three 7^1/$_4$" squares. Cut squares diagonally in quarters to make 24 geese. Cut each sky fabric into 24 squares 3^7/$_8$". Cut squares diagonally in half to make 48 sky triangles.

2. Use a ^{1}/$_4$" seam to sew a sky triangle to each goose. Press seam toward sky fabric. Repeat for second sky. Sew all sky triangles to geese. Trim rectangles to 3^1/$_2$" x 6^1/$_2$".

3. Arrange geese in 2 rows of 12. Sew rows together. Press.

4. Borders: Cut 2 long borders 2" x 36^1/$_2$". Add long borders. Press toward border. Cut 2 short borders 2" x 15^1/$_2$". Add short borders. Press toward border.

5. Layer the backing, batting and the assembled top. Baste all the layers together. Quilt as desired. Trim the batting even with the edges of the quilt top.

6. Sew binding strips together end to end. Stitch binding to quilt.

7. Collect leaves from your yard or use patterns provided. Trace leaves onto freezer paper. Press paper to wool. Cut out.

8. Applique leaves to quilt top with a Blanket stitch.

Add inner borders to center background. Press seams toward the border.

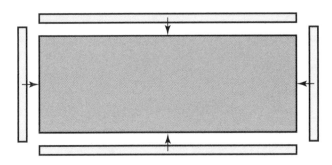

Sew long outer borders and then short outer borders to ends and press toward border.

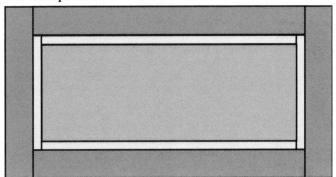

Matt's Cat in the Pumpkin Patch Table Runner

by Betsy Chutchian

Finished size: $16^{1}/_{2}$" x $41^{1}/_{2}$"

MATERIALS:
- Background: $3/8$ yd Blue plaid for center background
- Border: $1/8$ yd Gold stripe for inner border; $1/3$ yard Navy tone on tone for outer border
- Binding: 1 fat quarter Blue plaid for bias binding 18" x 22"
- Backing: $1/2$ yard Blue plaid
- Batting: 18" x 45"
- Brown homespun for vine 8" x 8"
- Variety of Orange and Rust felted wool for pumpkins
- Green felted wool for leaves and squiggles 5" x 8"
- Brown felted wool for stems 6" x 6"
- Black felted wool for cat 7" x 11"
- *DMC* size 8 Perle cotton (Blue #930, Rust #434, Orange #919, Green #94, Taupe #840, Black #310)

INSTRUCTIONS:

1. Cut Blue plaid center background $11^{1}/_{2}$" x $36^{1}/_{2}$". Cut 2 pieces of Gold stripe inner border 1" x $36^{1}/_{2}$". Use $1/4$" seams to sew the Gold stripe to the long sides of the Blue plaid. Press toward the border.

2. Cut 2 pieces of Gold stripe inner border 1" x $12^{1}/_{2}$". Use $1/4$" seams to sew the Gold stripe to the short sides of the Blue plaid. Press toward border.

3. Cut 2 pieces of Navy outer border $2^{1}/_{2}$" x $37^{1}/_{2}$". Sew to the long sides. Press toward border. Cut 2 pieces of Navy outer border $2^{1}/_{2}$" x $16^{1}/_{2}$". Sew to the short sides. Press toward border.

4. Trace 2 leaves, 1 cat, 5 pumpkins and 5 stems onto fusible web. Press to wool. Cut out shapes. Cut 4 squiggles on the bias $1/4$" wide. Blanket stitch shapes in place. Attach squiggles with a Running stitch. Save leaf veins and pumpkin creases for quilting.

5. Baste layers together. Hand or machine quilt, details in shapes.

6. Binding: Cut 3 strips $2^{1}/_{2}$" x 44". Join the ends of the strips together. Fold in half lengthwise. With raw edges together, sew the binding to the quilt using a $1/4$" seam. Fold the binding over to back and sew down by hand or using a Blind stitch.

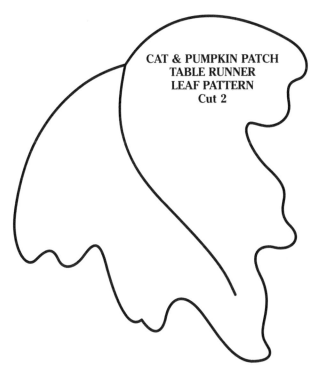

CAT & PUMPKIN PATCH TABLE RUNNER LEAF PATTERN Cut 2

Table Runner Patterns continued on pages 64 - 69

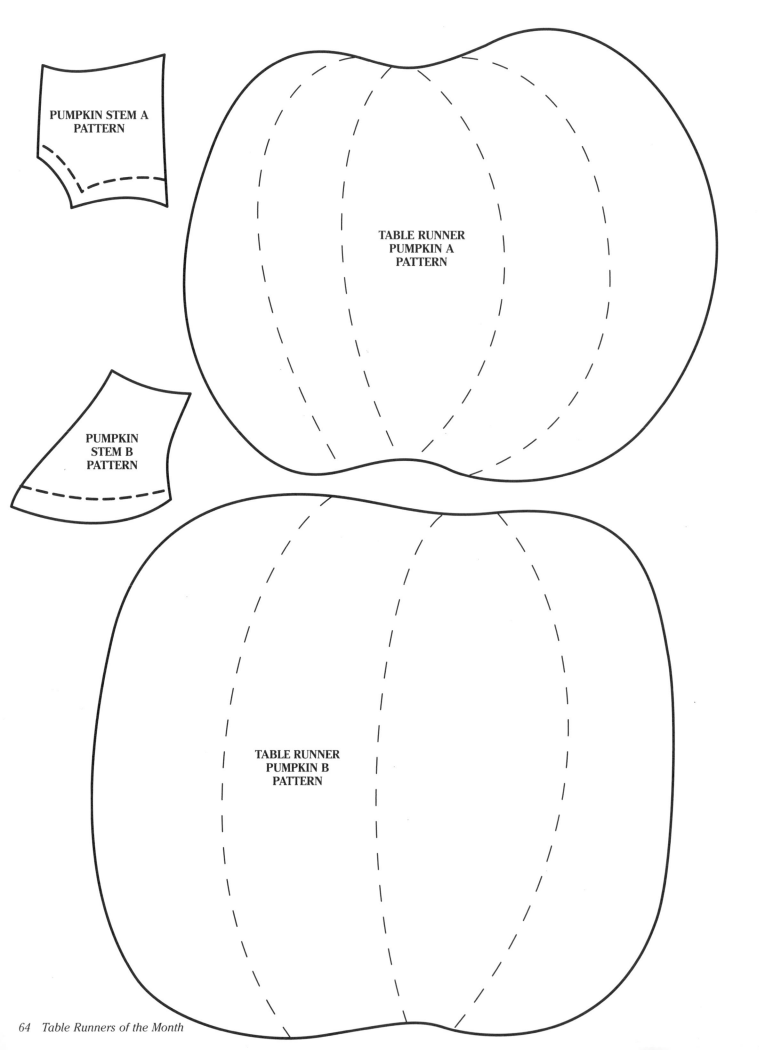

PUMPKIN STEM A
PATTERN

TABLE RUNNER
PUMPKIN A
PATTERN

PUMPKIN
STEM B
PATTERN

TABLE RUNNER
PUMPKIN B
PATTERN

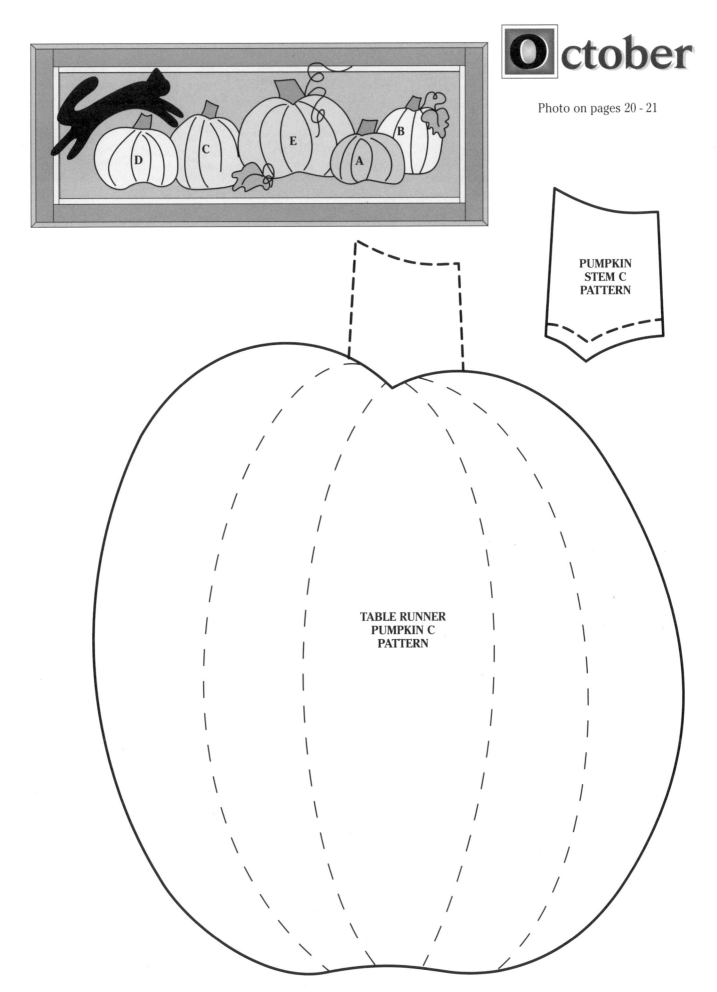

Photo on pages 20 - 21

**PUMPKIN
STEM C
PATTERN**

**TABLE RUNNER
PUMPKIN C
PATTERN**

Placemat and Napkins

by Betsy Chutchian

Finished sizes: Placemat: 14" x 16", Napkins: 18" square

MATERIALS for set of 4:
- 8 fat quarters of Orange plaid homespun or brushed cotton, or 4 pieces 1/2 yard each, or 2 pieces 1 yard each for placemats
- 1 yard napkin fabric cut into 4 squares (18" x 18")
- Brown felted wool for stems (6" x 12")
- *DMC* Rust size 8 Perle cotton or embroidery floss
- 1/2 yard Hobbs Heirloom 96" wide batting

INSTRUCTIONS:

1. Trace the giant pumpkin from the pattern given onto freezer paper. Press. Cut out 8. Trace the stems and cut out 2 layers of wool for each of the 4 stems.

2. With right sides together, layer pumpkins with batting on the bottom.

3. Sew through all layers with a 1/4" seam, leaving an opening at the stem area for turning.

4. After stitching, trim seam to 1/8". Turn right side out, rounding out seams.

5. Insert 2 layers of stem wool. Turn under stem opening and pin in place.

   Stitch opening closed. Blanket stitch around the stem with Rust Perle cotton.

6. Press placemat. Mark creases on pumpkin and quilt a Running stitch through all layers.

   Also quilt a Running stitch around the outer edge 1/4" from the seam.

7. To make napkins, serge edges or fold over 1/4" hem twice, mitering the corners. Press and hem with a Running stitch, Cross stitch, or Blanket stitch.

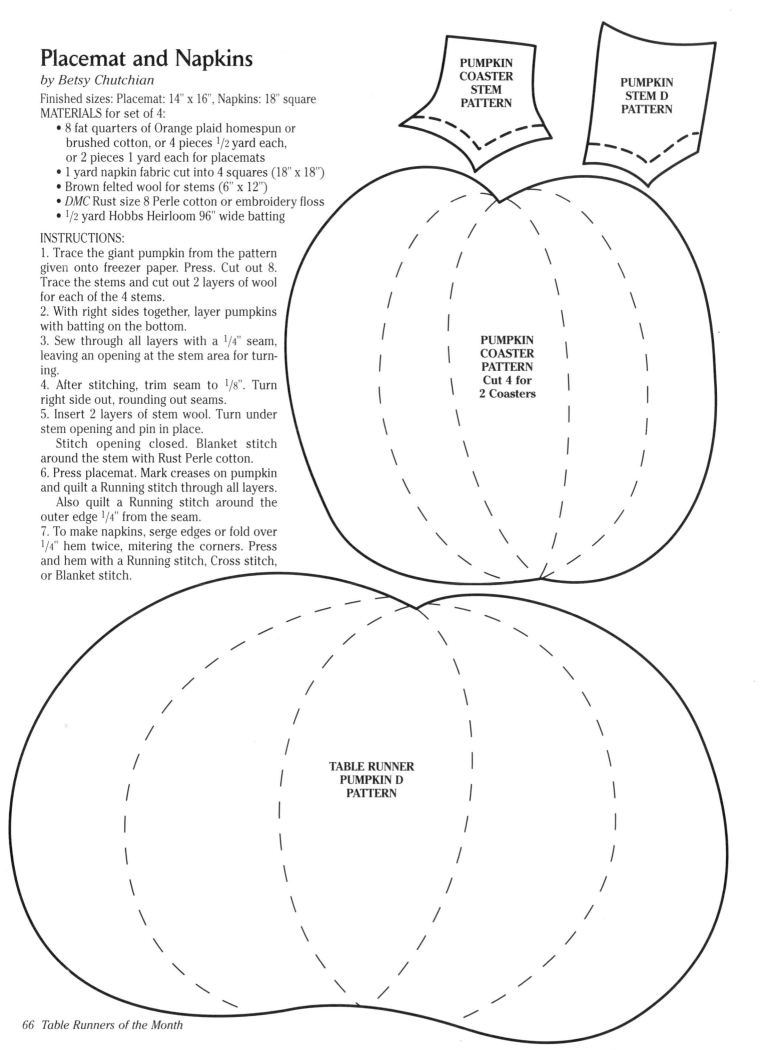

PUMPKIN COASTER STEM PATTERN

PUMPKIN STEM D PATTERN

PUMPKIN COASTER PATTERN
Cut 4 for 2 Coasters

TABLE RUNNER PUMPKIN D PATTERN

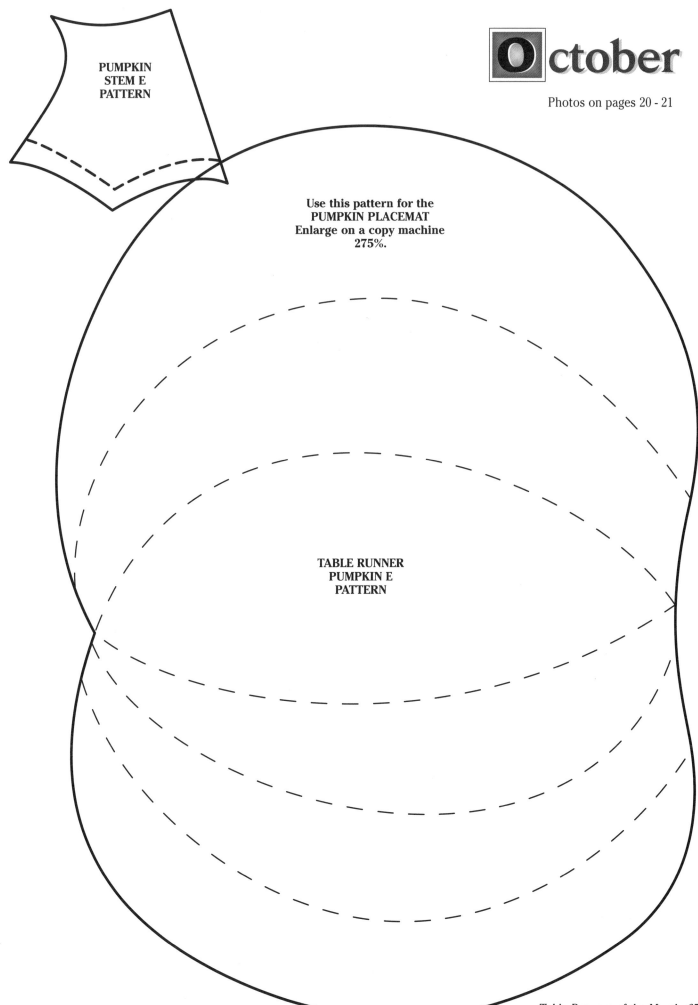

PUMPKIN
STEM E
PATTERN

Use this pattern for the
PUMPKIN PLACEMAT
Enlarge on a copy machine
275%.

**TABLE RUNNER
PUMPKIN E
PATTERN**

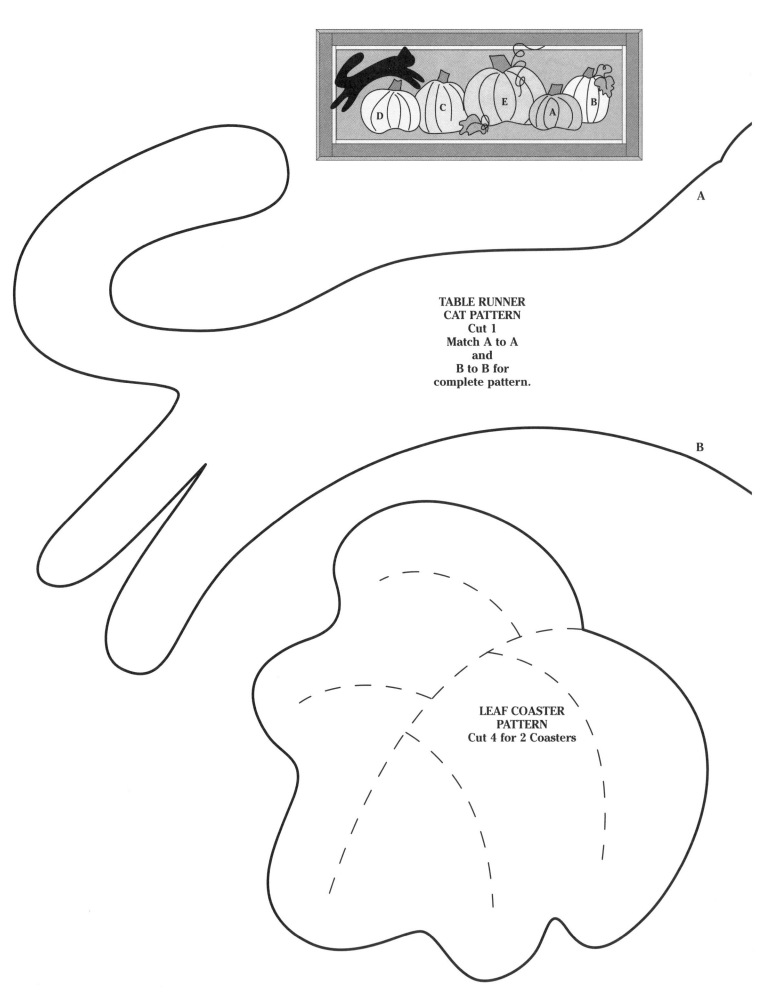

**TABLE RUNNER
CAT PATTERN
Cut 1
Match A to A
and
B to B for
complete pattern.**

A

B

**LEAF COASTER
PATTERN
Cut 4 for 2 Coasters**

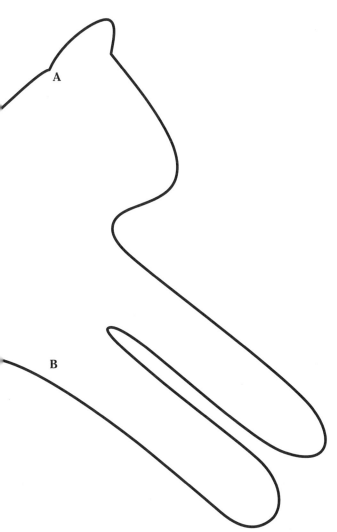

A

B

Pumpkin Pincushion
by Betsy Chutchian

Finished size: 2" tall x 4¹/₄" diameter

MATERIALS:
- Pumpkin colored felted wool (5" x 9") for top/bottom and (2" x 14") for side
- Brown or Green felted wool for stem (2" square)
- Wool or cotton stuffing
- *DMC* size 7 Perle cotton or embroidery floss to match wool
- Plastic coated freezer paper
- Cardboard circle 4" in diameter

INSTRUCTIONS:
1. Trace the circle pattern for the pincushion onto freezer paper. Transfer shape to wool. Cut out 2 circles.
2. Trace and cut out 2 stems. Blanket stitch the stems together.
3. Use a Blanket stitch and Perle cotton to stitch the side to the bottom circle. The ends will overlap. Close the side seam with a Blanket stitch.
4. Insert the cardboard circle. Blanket stitch the top circles to the side, leaving a 2" opening for stuffing.
5. Stuff the pincushion. Close opening with a Blanket stitch.

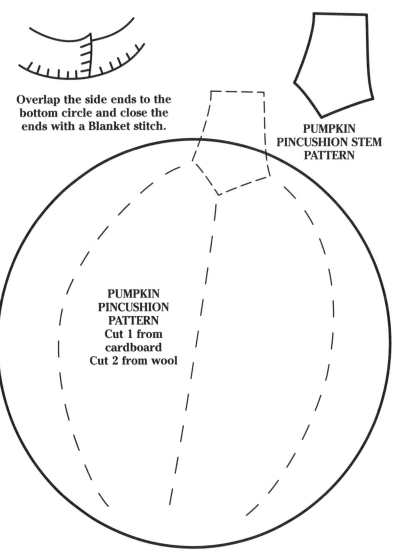

Overlap the side ends to the bottom circle and close the ends with a Blanket stitch.

PUMPKIN PINCUSHION STEM PATTERN

PUMPKIN PINCUSHION PATTERN
Cut 1 from cardboard
Cut 2 from wool

Pumpkin & Leaf Coasters
(not pictured)   *by Betsy Chutchian*

MATERIALS for 2 Pumpkin and 2 Leaf coasters:
- 2 pieces of Pumpkin colored felted wool (10" square)
- 2 pieces of Brown or Green felted wool for stems (4" square)
- 2 pieces of Green felted wool for leaves (5" x 10")
- *DMC* size 8 Perle cotton or embroidery floss to match wool
- Plastic coated freezer paper

INSTRUCTIONS:
1. Trace shapes onto freezer paper. Cut out. Press onto wool. Pairs of wool shapes must be cut because a front and back will be sewn together.
2. Pin pumpkin shapes together with 2 stem pieces placed in between. Pin pairs of leaves together.
3. Blanket stitch around the outside edges.
4. Draw details in pumpkins and leaf veins. Sew a Running stitch through all layers.

Table Runner Construction

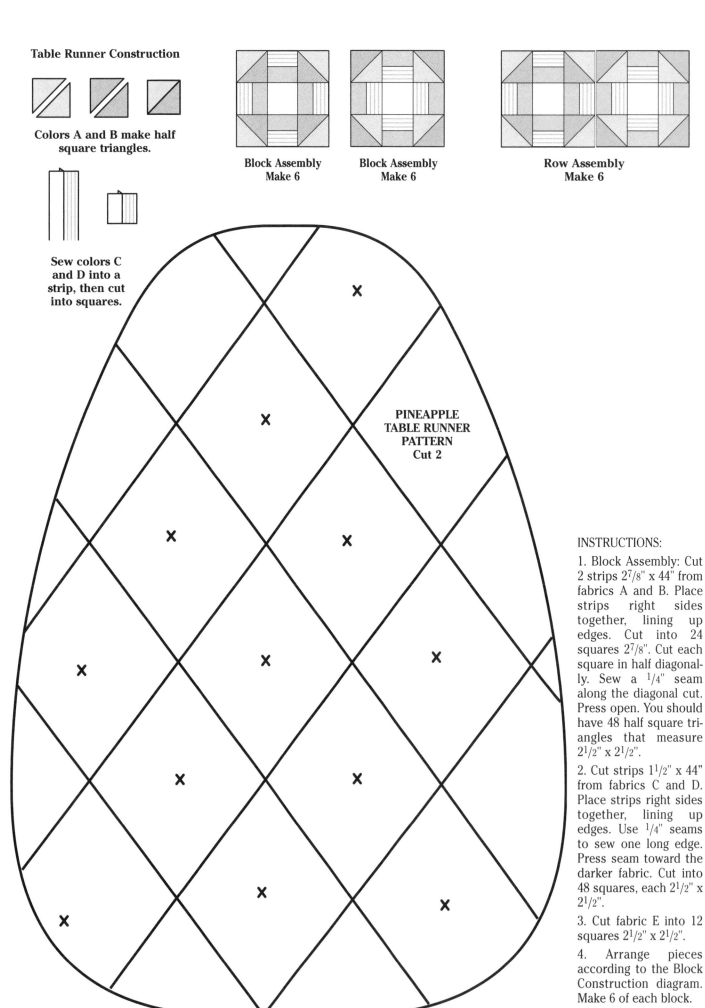

Colors A and B make half square triangles.

Sew colors C and D into a strip, then cut into squares.

Block Assembly
Make 6

Block Assembly
Make 6

Row Assembly
Make 6

PINEAPPLE
TABLE RUNNER
PATTERN
Cut 2

INSTRUCTIONS:

1. Block Assembly: Cut 2 strips $2^7/8$" x 44" from fabrics A and B. Place strips right sides together, lining up edges. Cut into 24 squares $2^7/8$". Cut each square in half diagonally. Sew a $1/4$" seam along the diagonal cut. Press open. You should have 48 half square triangles that measure $2^1/2$" x $2^1/2$".

2. Cut strips $1^1/2$" x 44" from fabrics C and D. Place strips right sides together, lining up edges. Use $1/4$" seams to sew one long edge. Press seam toward the darker fabric. Cut into 48 squares, each $2^1/2$" x $2^1/2$".

3. Cut fabric E into 12 squares $2^1/2$" x $2^1/2$".

4. Arrange pieces according to the Block Construction diagram. Make 6 of each block.

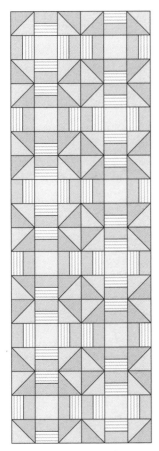

**Sew Rows Together -
Alternate blocks in each row**

Border Assembly

Photo on page 25

Hospitality Table Runner
by Betty Edgell

Finished size: 16^1/$_2$" x 40^1/$_2$"

MATERIALS:
- Background: ^{3}/$_8$ yd each of 2 Tan fabrics, light A and darker B for half square triangles
- 1 fat quarter each of 2 Tan fabrics, darker C and lighter D, for rectangles
- ^{1}/$_8$ yd Tan fabric labeled E for center square
- Border: ^{1}/$_4$ yard (Sample used fabric E.)
- Binding: ^{1}/$_4$ yard (2^1/$_2$" by width of fabric strips)
- Backing: ^{1}/$_2$ yard
- Batting: 18" x 45"
- Gold felted wool (12" x 15")
- Green felted wool (6" x 12")
- *DMC* size 8 Ecru, Golden and Green Perle cotton or 3 strands embroidery floss to match wool
- Plastic coated freezer paper

5. See Block placement diagram. Sew 6 rows of 2. Press seams in opposite directions on alternating rows.

6. Cut 2 long border strips 2^1/$_2$" x 36^1/$_2$". Add long borders. Press toward border.

7. Cut 2 short border strips 2^1/$_2$" x 16^1/$_2$". Add short borders. Press toward border.

8. Trace pineapple and leaf onto freezer paper. Press to wool. Cut out shapes. Baste in place. Blanket stitch around appliques. Save the diagonal lines and "x's" in the pattern for quilting.

9. Layer backing, batting, and quilt top. Baste. Quilt as desired.

10. Cut 3 bias strips 2^1/$_2$" wide. Join the ends of the strips together. Fold in half lengthwise. With raw edges together, sew the binding to the quilt using a ^{1}/$_4$" seam. Miter the corners. Fold the binding over and sew down by hand or machine.

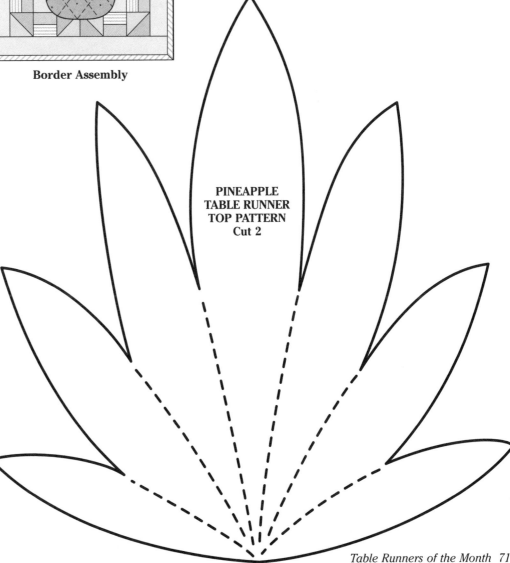

**PINEAPPLE
TABLE RUNNER
TOP PATTERN
Cut 2**

Hospitality Tea Cozy

by Betty Edgell

Finished Size: 10" x 12¹/₂"

MATERIALS:
- Green felted wool for leaves (5" square)
- Brown felted wool for pineapple (5" square)
- Medium Brown fabric for outside (18" x 22")
- Light Brown fabric for inside lining (18" x 22")
- Light Brown print or coordinating fabric for bias binding (18" x 22")
- Batting (18" square)
- *DMC* size 8 Perle cotton or embroidery floss to match wool
- Plastic coated freezer paper

INSTRUCTIONS:

1. Place batting between outside fabric and lining fabric. Machine quilt.

2. Trace cozy pattern onto freezer paper.

3. Press shiny side of freezer paper onto quilted square.

4. Cut out front and back pieces, adding ¹/₂" seam allowance.

5. Cut binding into 2¹/₄" wide bias strips. Join strips together to make one strip for the curve and one strip for bottom of cozy. Fold bias strips in half and press.

6. Trace shapes onto freezer paper, press onto wool. Cut out shapes.

7. Center shapes on outside of cozy and Blanket stitch in place.

8. Place two sides of cozy together, right sides out. Sew a generous ¹/₄" seam along curve, leaving bottom open.

9. Machine sew binding to one side of curve. Fold binding over curved edge and attach by hand to the other side.

10. Sew binding to bottom edge of cozy using the same technique

HOSPITALITY TEA COZY PATTERNS

Fold

Photo on page 24

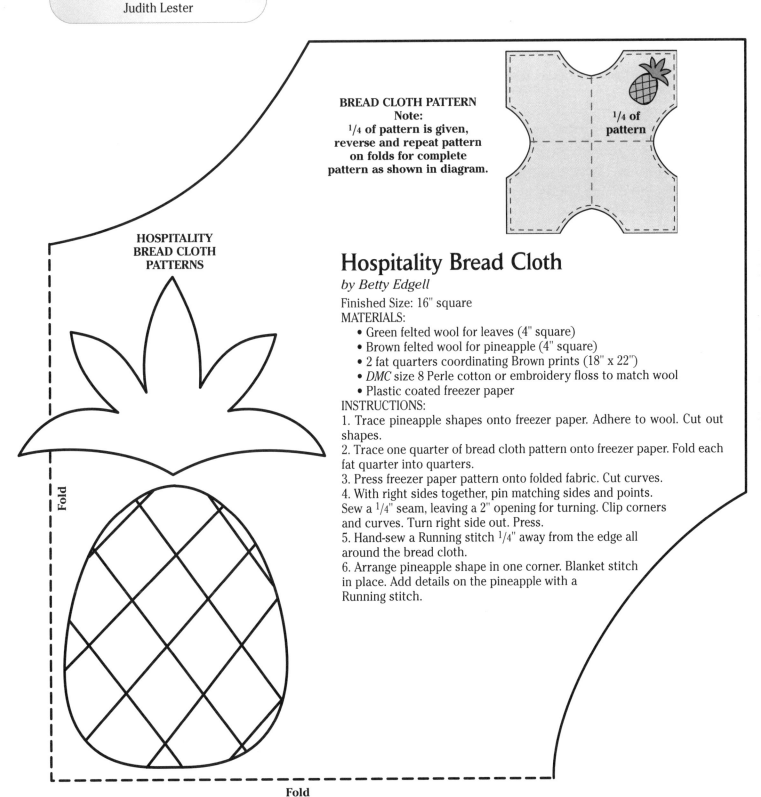

BREAD CLOTH PATTERN
Note:
1/4 of pattern is given, reverse and repeat pattern on folds for complete pattern as shown in diagram.

1/4 of pattern

HOSPITALITY BREAD CLOTH PATTERNS

Fold

Fold

Hospitality Bread Cloth

by Betty Edgell

Finished Size: 16" square

MATERIALS:
- Green felted wool for leaves (4" square)
- Brown felted wool for pineapple (4" square)
- 2 fat quarters coordinating Brown prints (18" x 22")
- *DMC* size 8 Perle cotton or embroidery floss to match wool
- Plastic coated freezer paper

INSTRUCTIONS:
1. Trace pineapple shapes onto freezer paper. Adhere to wool. Cut out shapes.
2. Trace one quarter of bread cloth pattern onto freezer paper. Fold each fat quarter into quarters.
3. Press freezer paper pattern onto folded fabric. Cut curves.
4. With right sides together, pin matching sides and points. Sew a 1/4" seam, leaving a 2" opening for turning. Clip corners and curves. Turn right side out. Press.
5. Hand-sew a Running stitch 1/4" away from the edge all around the bread cloth.
6. Arrange pineapple shape in one corner. Blanket stitch in place. Add details on the pineapple with a Running stitch.

Diagrams for Piecing Table Runner

| 1 | 3 | 5 | 7 | White |
| 2 | 4 | 6 | 8 | Cream |

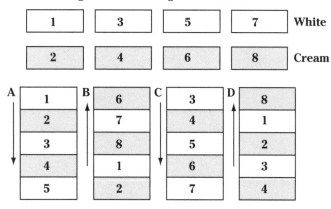

A 1 2 3 4 5 **B** 6 7 8 1 2 **C** 3 4 5 6 7 **D** 8 1 2 3 4

Arrows indicate the pressing direction.

E 5 6 7 8 1 **F** 2 3 4 5 6 **G** 7 8 1 2 3 **H** 4 5 6 7 8

Row Assembly

Sew strips together.

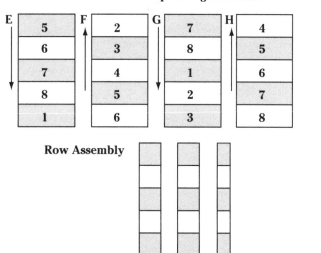

	A	B	C	D	E	F	G	H	A	B	C	D	E	F	G	H
1	6	3	8	5	2	7	4	1	6	3	8	5	2	7	4
2	7	4	1	6	3	8	5	2	7	4	1	6	3	8	5
3	8	5	2	7	4	1	6	3	8	5	2	7	4	1	6
4	1	6	3	8	5	2	7	4	1	6	3	8	5	2	7
5	2	7	4	1	6	3	8	5	2	7	4	1	6	3	8

Add long borders and then short borders.

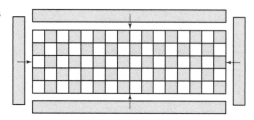

Holly Berry Table Runner

by Betsy Chutchian

Finished size: $14^{1}/_{2}$" x $36^{1}/_{2}$"

MATERIALS:
- Background: $^{1}/_{6}$ yd each of 4 shades of White labeled 1, 3, 5, 7 and 4 shades of Cream labeled 2, 4, 6, and 8 (6" x 45")
- Border and Binding: $^{1}/_{2}$ yard Cream 18" x 45"
- Backing: $^{1}/_{2}$ yard Cream 18" x 45"
- Batting: 18" x 45"
- 1 fat quarter Brown homespun for vine (18" x 22")
- Green felted wool (12" x 16")
- Red felted wool (4" x 6")
- *DMC* size 8 Ecru, Red #115, and Green #890 Perle cotton for hand applique and hand quilting

INSTRUCTIONS:

1. From each White and Cream, cut 1 strip $2^{1}/_{2}$" x 28". Cut each strip into 4 pieces $2^{1}/_{2}$" x 7". Label each strip 1-8.

2. Arrange sets of strips labeled A through H according to the diagram. Arrows indicate pressing direction. Use $^{1}/_{4}$" seams to sew the sets together. From each set cut 2 strips $2^{1}/_{2}$". Sew the strips together according to the diagram. Press.

3. Cut 2 Cream long borders $2^{1}/_{2}$" x $32^{1}/_{2}$". Add long borders. Press the seam toward the border.

4. Cut 2 Cream short borders $2^{1}/_{2}$" x $14^{1}/_{2}$". Add the short border. Press the seam toward the border.

5. Cut bias strips of homespun $^{7}/_{8}$" wide. Fold each edge $^{1}/_{4}$" under to make a finished vine of $^{3}/_{8}$" x 28". Blind stitch vine in place.

6. Trace applique shapes. Transfer to wool. Cut out shapes. Blanket stitch in place.

7. Baste layers together. Hand or machine quilt in diagonal lines.

8. Cut 3 strips $2^{1}/_{2}$" x 44". Join the ends of the strips together. Fold in half lengthwise. With raw edges together, sew the binding to the quilt using a $^{1}/_{4}$" seam. Miter the corners. Fold the binding over and sew down by hand or with Blind stitch.

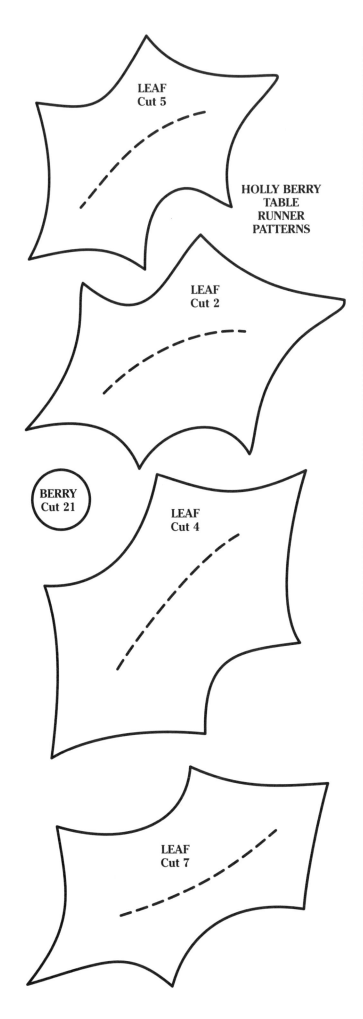

LEAF
Cut 5

HOLLY BERRY
TABLE
RUNNER
PATTERNS

LEAF
Cut 2

BERRY
Cut 21

LEAF
Cut 4

LEAF
Cut 7

December
Holly Berry
Photo on page 24

Holly Berry Slippers

by Betsy Chutchian

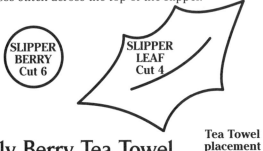

MATERIALS:
- 1 pair of purchased Black slippers
- Red felted wool (4" square)
- Green felted wool (5" square)
- *DMC* Red and Green size 8 Perle cotton
- Large eye sharp needle
- Plastic coated freezer paper

INSTRUCTIONS:
1. Trace patterns and transfer to wool. Iron patterns onto felt. Cut out 6 berries and 4 leaves.
2. Whipstitch leaves and berries to the slippers with Perle cotton.

   The stitches do not go all the way through the slipper fabric.
3. Use Red Perle cotton to stitch diagonal lines around the edge of the slipper opening.

   Cross stitch across the top of the slipper.

SLIPPER
BERRY
Cut 6

SLIPPER
LEAF
Cut 4

Holly Berry Tea Towel

Tea Towel placement diagram

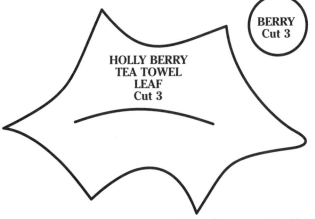

by Betsy Chutchian

MATERIALS:
- 1 purchased Red or Green tea towel with an open area for embroidery
- *DMC* Red and Green size 8 Perle cotton or 3 strands embroidery floss
- Freezer paper or light box to trace design

INSTRUCTIONS:
1. Trace 2 leaves and 3 berries onto tea towel.
2. Embroider design.

BERRY
Cut 3

HOLLY BERRY
TEA TOWEL
LEAF
Cut 3

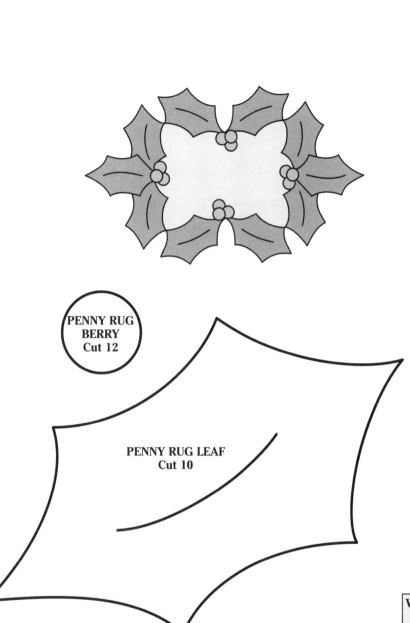

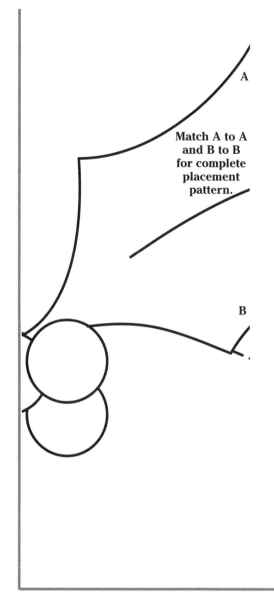

Match A to A and B to B for complete placement pattern.

PENNY RUG BERRY
Cut 12

PENNY RUG LEAF
Cut 10

Holly Berry Penny Rug

by Betsy Chutchian

Finished Size: 12" x 19"

MATERIALS:
- Background: White coat weight felted wool (13" x 20")
- Leaves: Dark Green felted wool (12" x 16")
- Berries: Red felted wool (4" x 6")
- *DMC* Red and Green size 8 Perle cotton or 3 strands embroidery floss
- Plastic coated freezer paper

INSTRUCTIONS:

1. Trace leaves and berries onto freezer paper. Cut out shapes. Press onto wool. Cut out.

2. Transfer Penny Rug pattern to White wool.

3. Use the pattern to arrange leaves and berries as shown in photo. Pin securely in place.

4. Trim White wool to meet edge of leaves.

5. Blanket stitch the outer edges of the leaves, sewing through all layers. Backstitch veins on leaves. Blanket stitch around the edges of the berries.

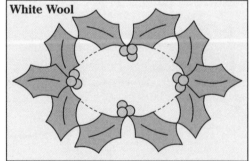

Trim White wool to meet edge of leaves.

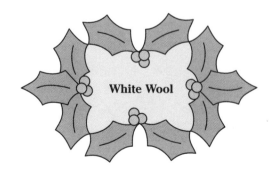

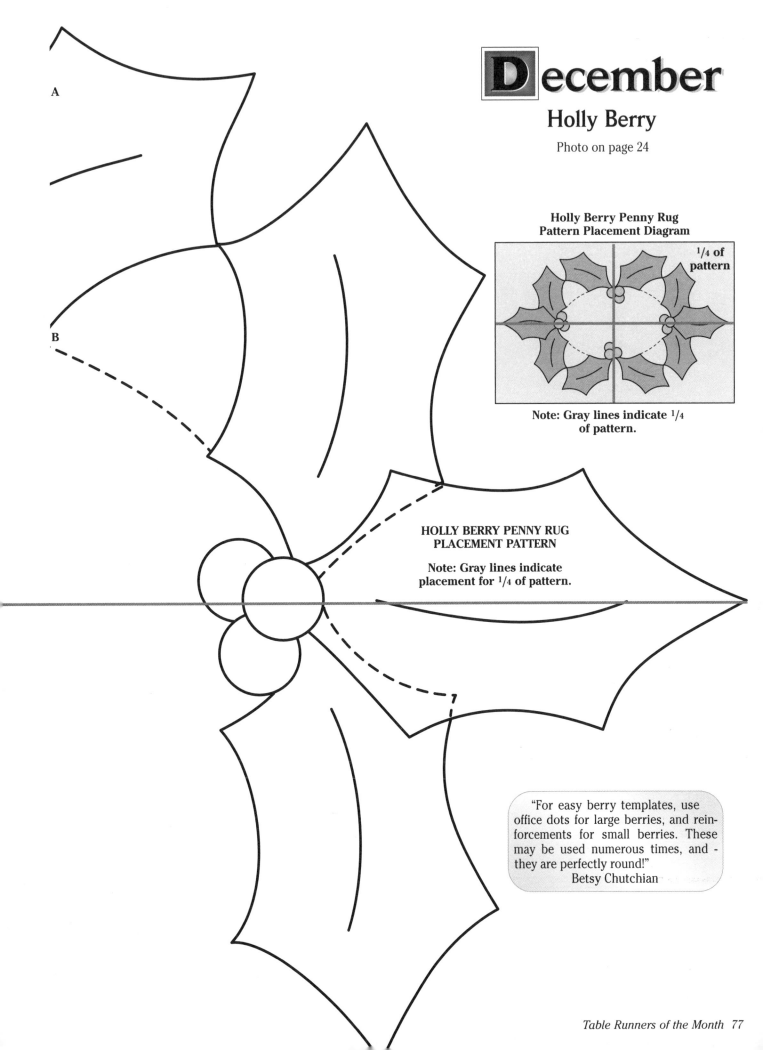

A

B

December

Holly Berry

Photo on page 24

**Holly Berry Penny Rug
Pattern Placement Diagram**

¹/4 **of
pattern**

Note: Gray lines indicate ¹/4
of pattern.

**HOLLY BERRY PENNY RUG
PLACEMENT PATTERN**

Note: Gray lines indicate
placement for ¹/4 of pattern.

"For easy berry templates, use
office dots for large berries, and rein-
forcements for small berries. These
may be used numerous times, and -
they are perfectly round!"
Betsy Chutchian

Seasonal Delights Quilt

by Betsy Chutchian, Betty Edgell, and Judith Lester
Quilted by Karen Roxbourgh

Finished Size: 60$\frac{1}{2}$" x 77"

This quilt is constructed in sections.

SECTION A: PRESS AFTER EACH SEAM.
1. Attach the first 3 rows of the Cupid's Arrow block to the Posy Basket. • 2. Attach the last row of Cupid's Arrow to the top row of the Watermelon block. • 3. Sew step 2 to the bottom of the Watermelon block. • 4. Sew step 1 to step 3. • 5. Sew the Hollyhock block to step 4. • 6. Complete applique as needed.

SECTION B: PRESS AFTER EACH SEAM.
1. Sew the top part of the Sunflower block to the Flying South block. • 2. Sew the bottom part of the Sunflower block to the Matt's Cat block • 3. Sew step 1 to step 2. • 4. Finish appliques as needed.• 5. Sew Section A to Section B.

SECTION C: PRESS AFTER EACH SEAM.
1. Sew the last row of the Morning Glory block to the lower Bunny block. • 2. Sew the Pineapple block to the Candle block. • 3. Sew Step 1 to Step 2. • 4. Sew section C to section A/B. • 5. Finish appliques as needed.

SECTION D: PRESS AFTER EACH SEAM.
1. Sew the Morning Glory block to the upper Bunny block. • 2. Sew the Snowflake block to step 1. • 3. Sew the Morning Glories square to Step 2. • 4. Sew Step 3 to Quilt section A/B/C. • 5. Finish applique as needed.
Quilt measures 44$\frac{1}{2}$" x 60$\frac{1}{2}$".

Quilt Block Construction of Sections

Continued on page 80.

Seasonal Delights Quilt

Seasonal Delights Quilt

Continued from page 79

Finished Size: 60$^1/_2$" x 77"

MATERIALS FOR BORDERS AND QUILT COMPLETION:
- $^1/_2$ yd Blue border fabric (inner border)
- $^3/_4$ yd Green brushed cotton for geese
- 2$^5/_8$ yds Blue marble fabric for outer border, geese, binding
- Backing: 5 yds print fabric for geese, outer border, backing, and binding
- Batting: 65" x 80"
- Green felted wool for the Hollyhock stem ($^7/_8$" x 45")
- Dark Green and Light Green felted wool for Hollyhock leaves and buds (6" square of each)
- Green felted wool for Hollyhock squiggles ($^1/_8$" x 12")
- Medium Pink felted wool for Hollyhock flowers (6" square)
- Light Pink felted wool for Hollyhock flowers (5" square)
- Yellow felted wool for Hollyhock flower centers (4" square)
- 1 fat quarter of Brown felted wool for Holly Berry vine (18" x 22")
- Green felted wool for Holly leaves (12" x 12")
- Red felted wool for Holly berries (6" x 6")
- Plastic coated freezer paper
- *DMC* size 8 Perle cotton or 3 strands embroidery floss to match wool

INSTRUCTIONS:

1. Cut 2 short Blue inner border strips 2$^1/_2$" x 44$^1/_2$". Cut 2 long borders 2$^1/_2$" x 65". Sew the short borders first. Press. Sew the long borders. Press. The quilt now measures 48$^1/_2$" x 65". • 2. Cut 11 squares from the goose fabric 7". Cut goose fabric square on the diagonal twice. Cut 44 squares of border print fabric 3$^7/_8$". Cut each square on the diagonal. • 3. See Block Construction diagram from Flying South block section B on page 90. Use a $^1/_4$" seam to sew the long side of a border triangle to the short side of a goose. Press seam toward border fabric. Repeat for second border triangle. Sew all border triangles to geese. Trim rectangles to 3$^1/_2$" x 6$^1/_2$". • 4. Sew a column of 10 geese for each side border. Sew a column of 12 geese for the top and bottom borders. Press. Cut 2 pieces of border fabric 6$^1/_2$" x 35" for the side columns. See photo for orientation of geese column on the right and left sides of the quilt. Sew a border piece to each geese column. It will measure 6$^1/_2$" x 65". Sew the left and right border pieces to the quilt. The quilt now measures 60$^1/_2$" x 65". • 5. Cut 2 pieces of border fabric 6$^1/_2$" x 24$^1/_2$" for the top and bottom. See photo for orientation of geese column for the top and bottom of the quilt. Sew a border piece to each geese column. It will measure 6$^1/_2$" x 65". Sew the top and bottom border pieces to the quilt. The quilt now measures 60$^1/_2$" x 77". • 6. Hollyhock Border Appliques: Trace patterns for hollyhock border onto freezer paper. Press onto wool. Cut out pieces. Arrange pieces according to the Border Placement diagram. Blanket stitch in place. • 7. Holly Berry Border Appliques: See Table Runner patterns on page 75. Trace pattern on freezer paper for 12 leaves and 12 berries. Press onto wool. Cut out shapes. Cut a bias vine $^3/_8$" wide. See photo for vine placement. Couch vine in place with a Cross stitch. Where seams on the vine join, cover with a leaf. Blanket stitch leaves in place. Berries are Straight stitched from the edge to the center. See Straight stitch diagram. • 8. Quilt Construction: Binding: Cut 7 strips across the width of the fabric 2$^1/_2$" wide. Sew strips together to make 285". Fold to 1$^1/_4$" wide. Press. Piece the backing to fit the quilt plus 2" on all sides. Layer backing, batting, and quilt top. Quilt as desired. Trim edges even. Add binding.

Cupid's Arrow Block Section A

Finished Size: 8$^1/_2$" x 12$^1/_2$" and 4$^1/_2$" x 8$^1/_2$"

MATERIALS:
- Background: 1 Cream fat quarter (18" x 22")
- Design: 8 different fat eighths of Red prints for arrows (4" x 8")
- 1 piece Red felted wool for hearts (8" x 8")
- *DMC* Red size 8 Perle cotton or 2 strands embroidery floss
- Plastic coated freezer paper

INSTRUCTIONS:

1. Cut 8 Cream 4" squares and cut them in half diagonally. Fold triangles in half.
2. From each Red print, cut 1 rectangle 1$^7/_8$" x 3$^1/_4$" and two 3" squares. Cut each square in half diagonally. Press in half. Fold and press the rectangle in half.
3. See diagrams for arrow block construction. Matching fold lines, place triangle over rectangle. Sew a $^1/_4$" seam. Press seam toward the Red fabric. Repeat with the second triangle. Trim Cream triangles even with the width of the Red rectangle. Match folds of Red triangle and Red rectangle. Sew a $^1/_4$" seam. Press seam toward the Red fabric. Repeat for second Red triangle.
4. Trim block to a 4$^1/_2$" square. If you prefer to construct this block with templates, a diagram has been provided.
5. Sew 2 blocks together according to the Block Assembly diagram. Press. Make 4 rows. Sew 3 rows together. Press.
   **You will not be able to sew the fourth row on until the watermelon section is completed.
6. Make a freezer paper pattern of the heart. Press onto wool. Cut out 2 hearts.
7. Use a Blanket stitch to applique the first heart in place. You will have to add the second heart after the watermelon section is added.

CUPID'S ARROW
HEART PATTERN

Seasonal Delights Quilt

Section A Quilt Block Construction

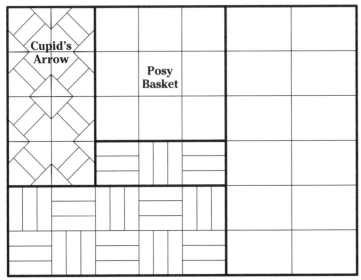

Cupid's Arrow Block Construction

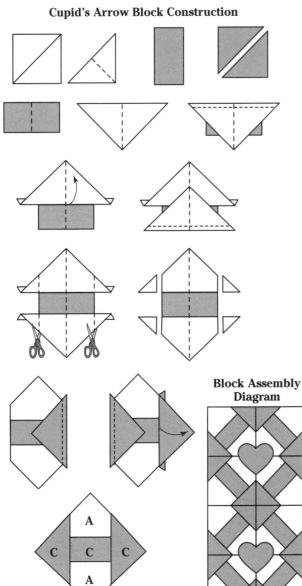

Block Assembly Diagram

Posy Basket Block Section A

Finished size: $12^{1}/_{2}$" square

MATERIALS:
- Background: $^{1}/_{8}$ yd of 3 different Pink fabrics labeled A, B, C (Three $4^{1}/_{2}$" squares from each)
- Coordinating print for basket (12" x 12")
- Felted wool for flowers: Yellow, Blue, Rose ($3^{1}/_{2}$" square each)
- Green print or felted wool for leaves: (6" square)
- *DMC* size 8 Perle cotton or 3 strands embroidery floss to match appliques
- Fusible web for applique pieces

INSTRUCTIONS:

1. Use $^{1}/_{4}$" seams to piece background Pink fabrics in 3 rows of 3. (See diagram.) Press seams in opposite directions on alternating rows. Sew the rows together. Press.

2. Trace patterns onto fusible web. Following manufacturer's directions, fuse and cut out shapes.

3. Place basket in the center of the block. Turn under edge and Blanket stitch. Arrange flowers and leaves. Blanket stitch in place. Add French Knots to flower centers.

Posy Basket Block Construction

A	B	C
C	A	B
B	C	A

Posy patterns on page 46

Watermelon Quilt Block
Section A

Finished Size: $8^1/_2$" x $20^1/_2$" and $4^1/_2$" x $12^1/_2$"

MATERIALS:
- Background: $^1/_6$ yd each Light Green, Medium Green, Dark Green (5" x 45")
- Red felted wool (12" x 12")
- Green felted wool (12" x 12")
- 15 small pieces Black or Brown felted wool for seeds (4" x 4")
- *DMC* size 8 Perle cotton or embroidery floss to match wool
- Plastic coated freezer paper

INSTRUCTIONS:
1. Cut each Green fabric into 2 strips $1^7/_8$" wide.
2. Use $^1/_4$" seam allowances to sew strips in order: Light, Medium, Dark. Press to dark.
3. Cut strips into 13 squares $4^1/_2$".
4. Piece together according to the diagram.
5. Trace patterns onto freezer paper. Press onto wool. Cut out pieces. Blanket stitch watermelon, rind, leaf and seeds. Stem stitch details on melon rind.
6. Cut a Green vine on the bias $^1/_4$" x 8". Applique using a Blanket stitch. (You won't be able to complete applique until top row is attached to bottom row of Cupid's Arrow.)

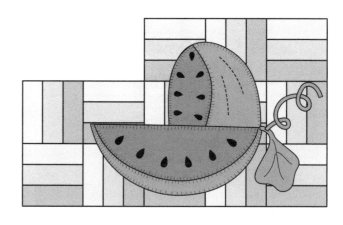

Section A Quilt Block Construction

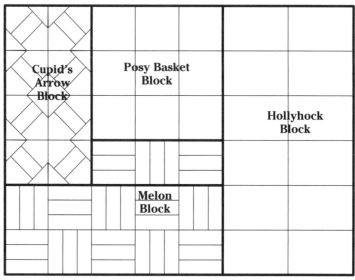

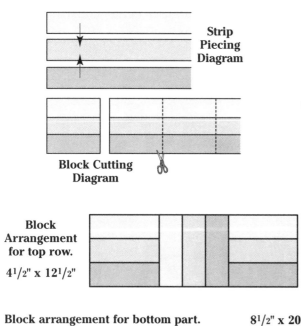

Strip Piecing Diagram

Block Cutting Diagram

Block Arrangement for top row.

$4^1/_2$" x $12^1/_2$"

Block arrangement for bottom part. $8^1/_2$" x $20^1/_2$"

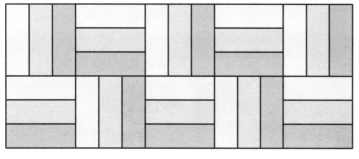

patterns on pages 48 - 50

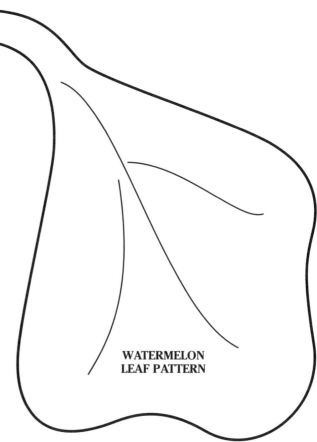

WATERMELON LEAF PATTERN

Seasonal Delights Quilt

Hollyhock Block Section A

Finished size: 12$\frac{1}{2}$" x 24$\frac{1}{2}$"

MATERIALS:
- Background: $\frac{1}{6}$ yd each of 2 shades of Cream with Blue print (5" x 45") labeled A and B
- 1 fat quarter Green brushed cotton for stems cut on bias (18" x 22")
- Pink felted wool for flowers (7" x 14")
- Green felted wool for leaves and buds (7" x 14")
- Yellow felted wool for flower center (5" square)
- *DMC* size 8 Pink, Green, and Yellow Perle cotton or 3 strand embroidery floss
- Plastic coated freezer paper

INSTRUCTIONS:
1. From each fabric A and B, cut 6 rectangles 4$\frac{1}{2}$" x 6$\frac{1}{2}$" • 2. Alternate rectangles A and B. (See diagram.) • Use $\frac{1}{4}$" seams. Sew 2 block sets together. Press the seams in different directions on alternate rows. Sew the rows together. • 3. Stems: Cut 3 bias strips from stem fabric 1$\frac{1}{2}$" wide. Cut left stem 1$\frac{1}{2}$" x 12". Cut the middle stem 1$\frac{1}{2}$" x 18". Cut the right stem 1$\frac{1}{2}$" x 16". Fold wrong sides together. Press. Arrange stems on the background. Blanket stitch in place. • 4. Trace flowers and leaves onto freezer paper. Press on wool. Cut out and baste in position. • Blanket stitch in place. • 5. See diagram for stitching buds above each stem. Each Straight stitch goes in the center and then outside the cut edge of the circle. Finish with a French Knot in the center.

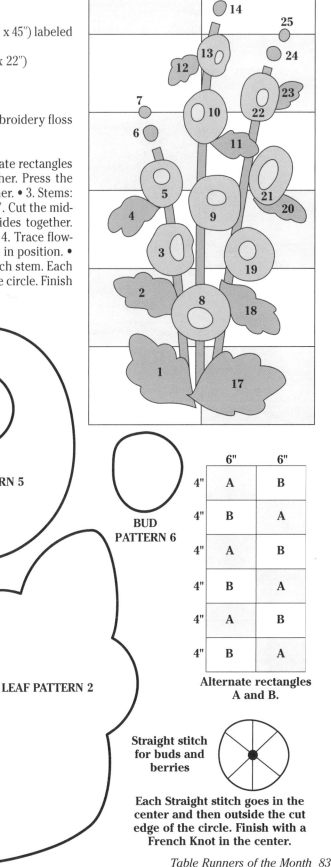

BUD PATTERN 7

FLOWER PATTERN 5

LEAF PATTERN 1

BUD PATTERN 6

LEAF PATTERN 2

	6"	6"
4"	A	B
4"	B	A
4"	A	B
4"	B	A
4"	A	B
4"	B	A

Alternate rectangles A and B.

Straight stitch for buds and berries

Each Straight stitch goes in the center and then outside the cut edge of the circle. Finish with a French Knot in the center.

Hollyhock Quilt Block Patterns continued on page 84

Hollyhock Block Section A

Patterns continued from page 83.

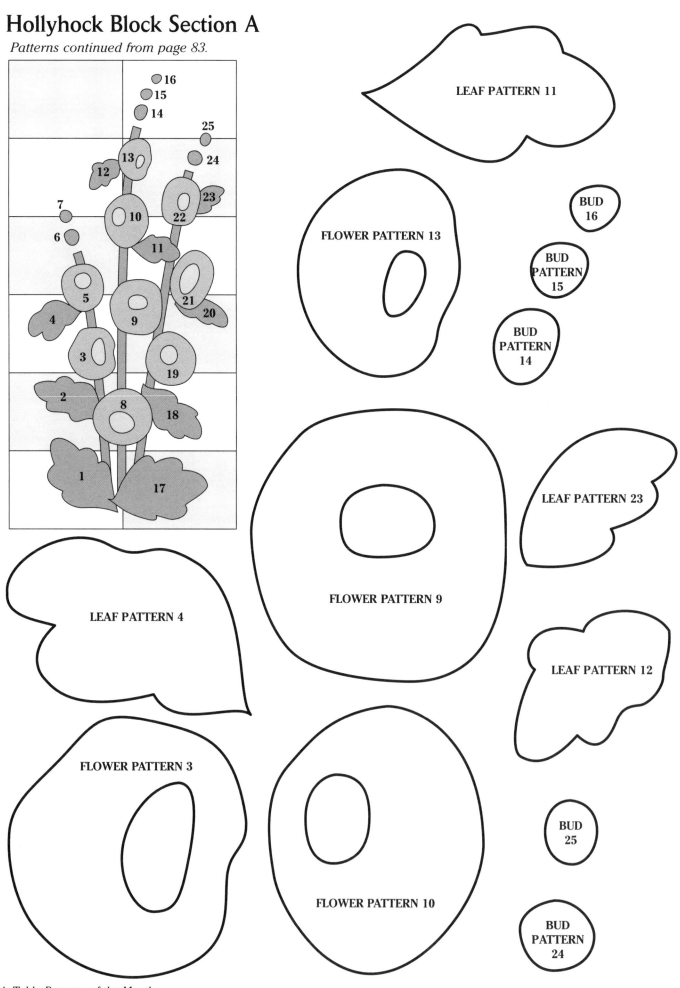

LEAF PATTERN 11

BUD 16

BUD PATTERN 15

FLOWER PATTERN 13

BUD PATTERN 14

LEAF PATTERN 23

FLOWER PATTERN 9

LEAF PATTERN 12

LEAF PATTERN 4

FLOWER PATTERN 3

FLOWER PATTERN 10

BUD 25

BUD PATTERN 24

Seasonal Delights Quilt

Hollyhock Block Section A

LEAF PATTERN 20

FLOWER PATTERN 8

FLOWER PATTERN 19

FLOWER PATTERN 21

LEAF PATTERN 18

LEAF PATTERN 17

FLOWER PATTERN 22

Sunflower Block Section B

Finished size: 12$^{1}/_{2}$" x 20$^{1}/_{2}$" and 8$^{1}/_{2}$" x 12$^{1}/_{2}$"

MATERIALS:
- Background: $^{1}/_{6}$ yard of each of the following fabrics (6" x 45"): Cream Light (A), Cream Medium (B), Tan Light(C), Tan Medium (D)
- 1 bucket fabric or wool (8" square)
- 1 fat quarter of Green brushed cotton for stems (18" x 22")
- Green felted wool for leaves and calyx (6$^{1}/_{2}$" x 13")
- Brown tweed felted wool for flower centers (3" x 5$^{1}/_{2}$")
- Yellow felted wool for flowers (9" square)
- *DMC* size 8 Brown, Green, Black and Yellow Perle cotton or 3 strand floss
- Plastic coated freezer paper

INSTRUCTIONS:

1. From fabrics A, B, C, and D, cut 6 squares 4$^{7}/_{8}$". • 2. To make half square triangles from fabrics A, B, C, and D, layer a light square on a dark square, right sides together. Draw a line on the diagonal. Sew a $^{1}/_{4}$" seam on each side of the line. Cut on the line. Press seam to the darker fabric. Trim to 4$^{1}/_{2}$". • 3. Use the Block Assembly diagrams to sew the half square triangles together. The 8$^{1}/_{2}$" x 12$^{1}/_{2}$" part will be sewn to the Matt's Cat block. The 12$^{1}/_{2}$" x 20$^{1}/_{2}$" part will be sewn to the Flying South block. Then the two pieces will be sewn together. • 4. You will not be able to applique until Section B of the quilt is assembled. Cut 3 Green bias stems 1$^{1}/_{2}$" wide in the following lengths: 12", 14", and 24". Fold each bias strip wrong sides together lengthwise and press. Stitch $^{1}/_{8}$" seam. • 5. Trace patterns for applique onto freezer paper. Cut out. Press onto fabric and wool. Cut out. Press under a $^{1}/_{4}$" hem around bucket. • 6. Arrange bucket, stems, and bottom leaf on background, overlapping bucket onto stems, and overlapping bottom leaf onto center stem. Baste in place. Fold bucket back to allow for sewing stems onto background and inside bucket. Stitch stems in place $^{1}/_{8}$" from raw edge. Fold stem over, hiding seam and raw edges. Applique stems in place. Baste bottom leaf in place. Blanket stitch around edge. Place top of bucket over stitched stems and bottom leaf. Blanket stitch in place. Arrange remaining pieces according to the photo. Blanket stitch appliques. Stem stitch the bucket handle. Add a Satin stitch to the bucket handle if desired. Flower centers are Satin stitched with a sewing machine in the sample, then Blanket stitched around the edge by hand.

Section B Quilt Block Construction

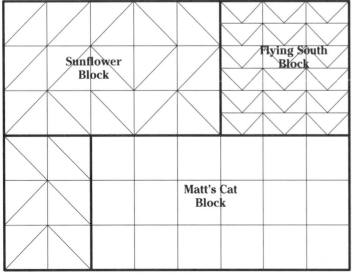

Sunflower Block Assembly Diagram

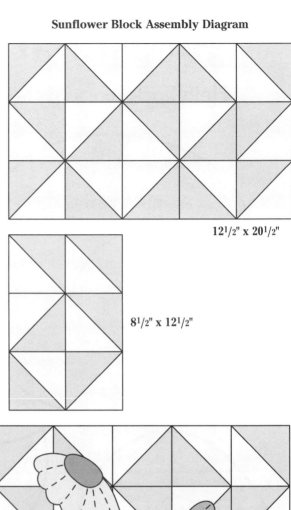

12$^{1}/_{2}$" x 20$^{1}/_{2}$"

8$^{1}/_{2}$" x 12$^{1}/_{2}$"

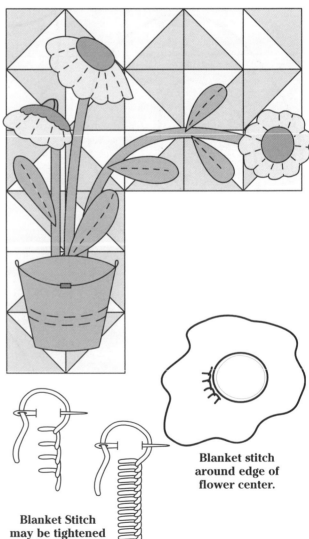

Blanket Stitch may be tightened up as needed.

Blanket stitch around edge of flower center.

Seasonal Delights Quilt

Sunflower Block Section B

MIDDLE FLOWER CENTER PATTERN
MIDDLE FLOWER PATTERN

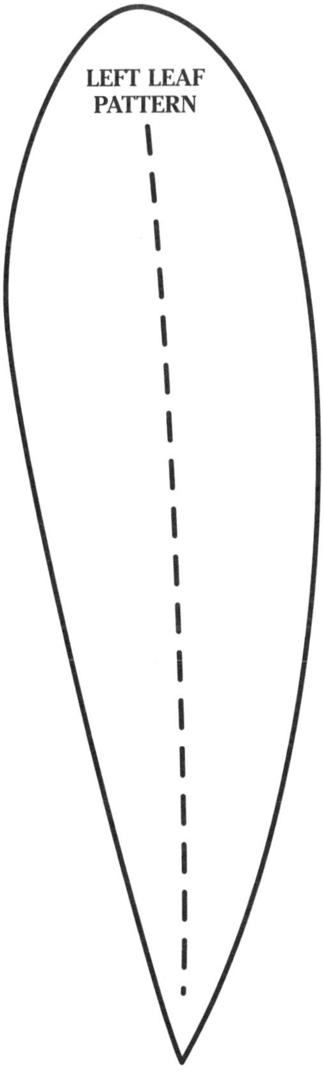

LEFT LEAF PATTERN

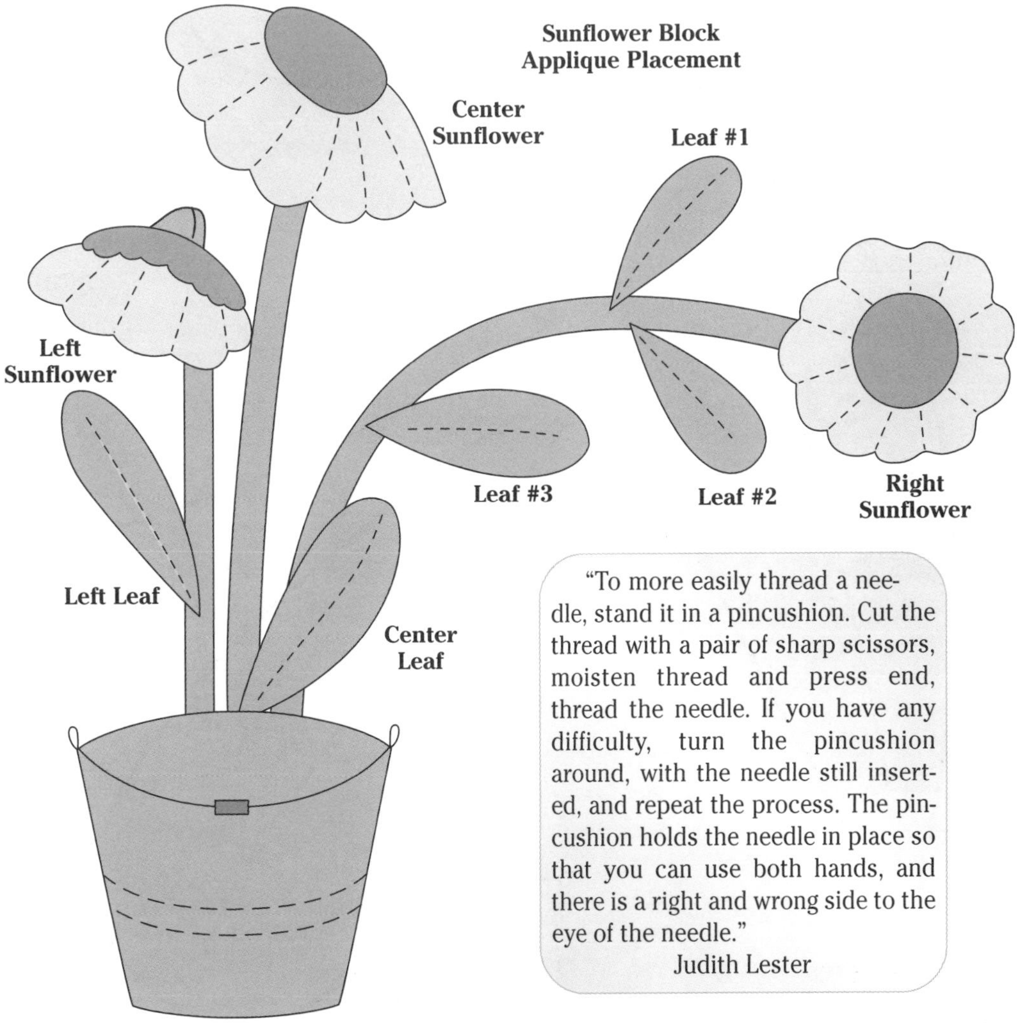

Sunflower Block Applique Placement
Center Sunflower
Leaf #1
Left Sunflower
Leaf #3
Leaf #2
Right Sunflower
Left Leaf
Center Leaf

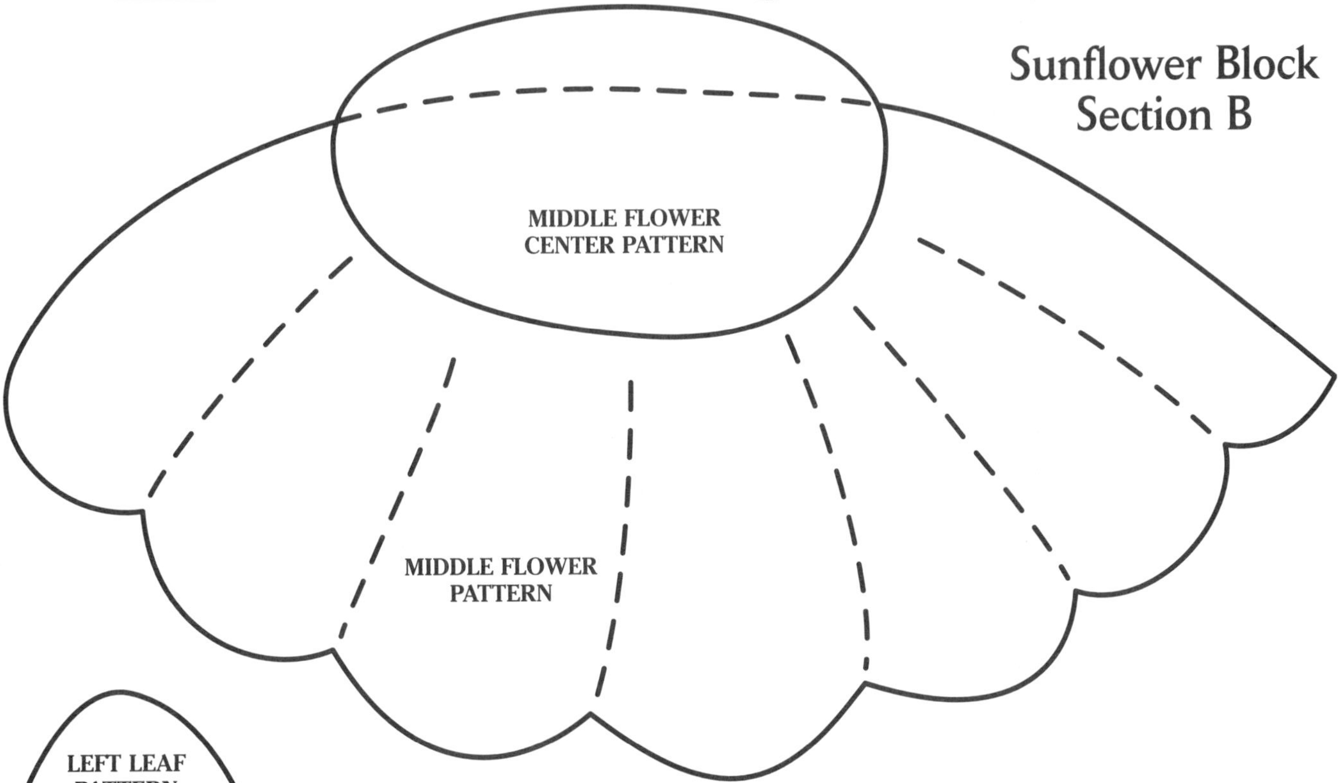

"To more easily thread a needle, stand it in a pincushion. Cut the thread with a pair of sharp scissors, moisten thread and press end, thread the needle. If you have any difficulty, turn the pincushion around, with the needle still inserted, and repeat the process. The pincushion holds the needle in place so that you can use both hands, and there is a right and wrong side to the eye of the needle."

Judith Lester

Sunflower Block Section B

Patterns continued from page 87.

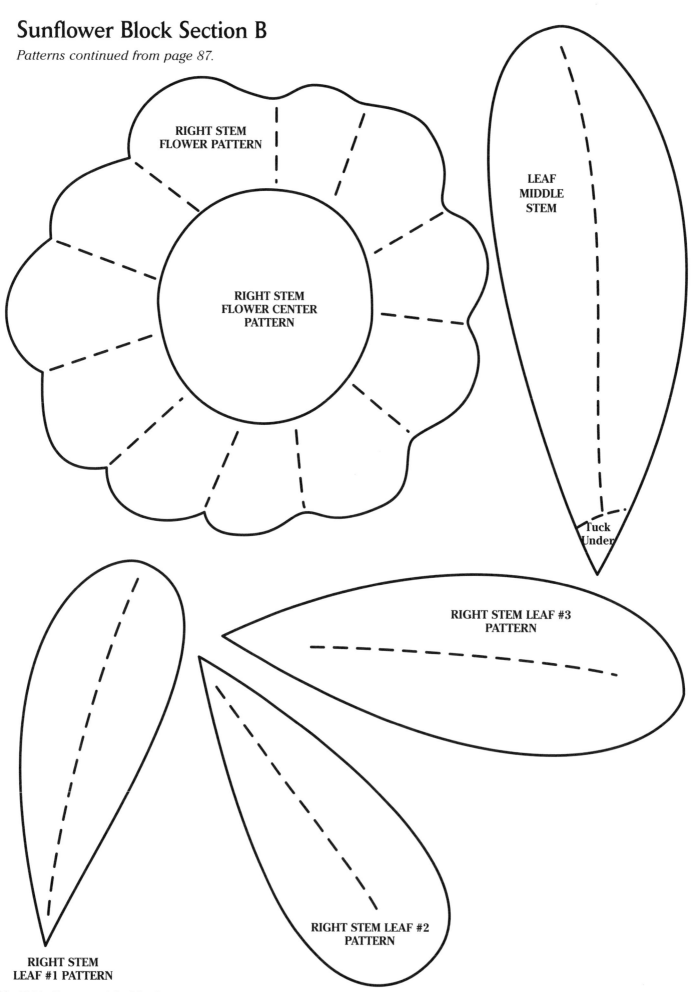

RIGHT STEM
FLOWER PATTERN

RIGHT STEM
FLOWER CENTER
PATTERN

LEAF
MIDDLE
STEM

Tuck
Under

RIGHT STEM LEAF #3
PATTERN

RIGHT STEM LEAF #2
PATTERN

RIGHT STEM
LEAF #1 PATTERN

Seasonal Delights Quilt

Sunflower Block Section B

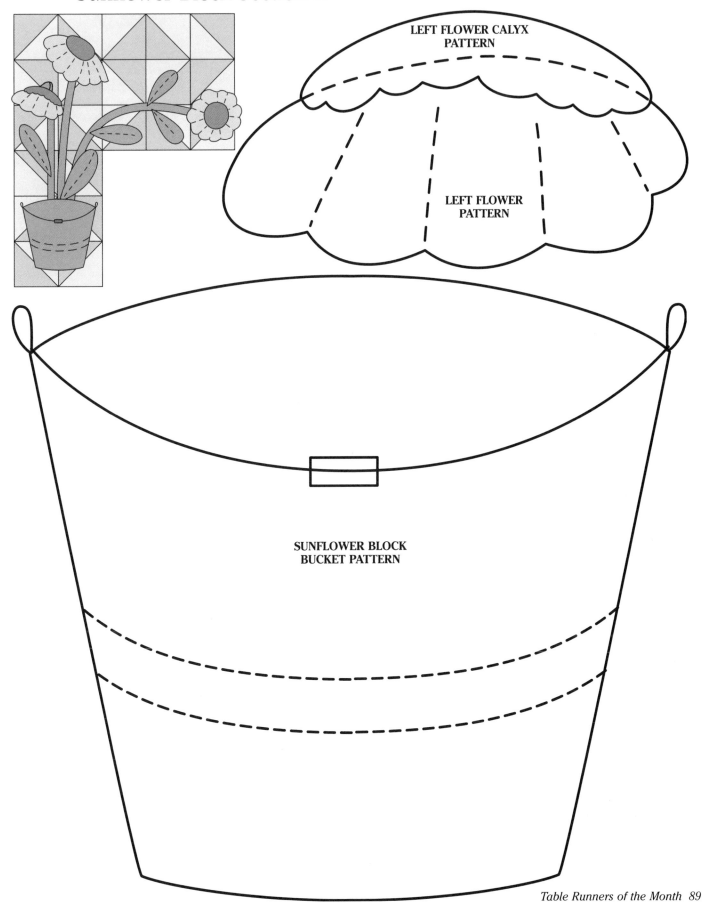

LEFT FLOWER CALYX
PATTERN

LEFT FLOWER
PATTERN

SUNFLOWER BLOCK
BUCKET PATTERN

Matt's Cat Block Section B

Finished size: $12^1/2$" x $24^1/2$"

MATERIALS:
- Background: $1/8$ yd each of 4 different Medium-Light Blue fabrics labeled A, B, C, and D.
- Pumpkin Orange felted wool (8" x 10" and 5" x 7")
- Green felted wool for leaves (4" x 8")
- Brown felted wool for stems and vine (5" x 5")
- Black felted wool for cat (6" x 12")
- *DMC* size 8 Perle cotton or 3 strands embroidery floss to match wool

INSTRUCTIONS:

1. Cut rectangles $4^1/2$" squares from the following fabrics: 4 A, 5 B, 5 C, 4 D. • 2. See Piecing Diagram. Use $1/4$" seams to make 3 rows of 6. • Press seams in opposite directions on alternating rows. • 3. The templates are the same as the Matt's Cat in the Pumpkin Patch Table Runner on pages 63-69. Trace pumpkins A and E, 2 leaves, 1 cat, and stems B and E onto freezer paper. Cut out. Press to wool and cut out. Cut 2 bias strips $1/8$" wide for squiggle vine from Brown wool. Blanket stitch

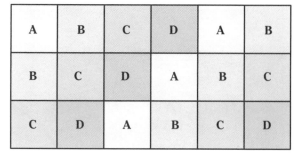

around shapes, leaving creases in the pumpkins and leaf details for the quilting. Stitch the squiggle stem with a Running stitch.

Matt's Cat Piecing Diagram

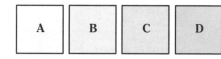

Flying South Block Section B

Finished Size: $12^1/2$" x $12^1/2$"

MATERIALS:
- Background: 2 fat quarters hand-dyed fabrics for geese (18" x 22")
- 2 fat quarters Blue hand-dyed fabrics for sky (18" x 22")
- 3 pieces Autumn Leaf colored felted wool 5" x 6"
- *DMC* size 8 Perle cotton to match leaf wool
- Plastic coated freezer paper

INSTRUCTIONS:

1. Cut each goose fabric into three $5^1/4$" squares. Cut squares diagonally in quarters to make 24 geese. Cut each sky fabric into 9 squares $2^7/8$". Cut squares diagonally in half to make 36 sky triangles. • 2. See Block Construction diagram. Use a $1/4$" seam to sew the long side of a sky triangle to the short side of a goose. Press seam toward sky fabric. Repeat for second sky triangle. Sew all sky triangles to geese. Trim rectangles to $2^1/2$" x $4^1/2$". • 3. See piecing diagram. Arrange geese in 6 rows of 3. Sew rows together. Press. • 4. Applique the leaves after Section B is assembled. • 5. Collect leaves from your yard or use pattern provided. Trace leaves onto freezer paper. Press paper to wool. Cut out. • 6. Applique leaves to quilt top with a Blanket stitch.

Section B Quilt Block Construction

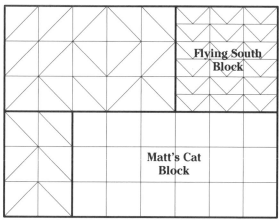

Flying South Block

Matt's Cat Block

Flying South Cutting Diagrams

Cut $5^1/4$" squares for geese. Quarter squares diagonally.

Cut $2^7/8$" squares for sky. Half squares diagonally.

Flying South Piecing Diagram

Flying South Applique Diagram

Flying South Block Construction

Note: This tail sticks out further than goose.

1. Stitch sky on dashed line.

2. Fold up sky.

3. Stitch sky on dashed line.

4. Fold up sky.

$\boxed{\text{S}}$easonal Delights Quilt

Morning Glory Block Section C

Finished size: 4¹/₂" x 12¹/₂" (bottom row)

MATERIALS:
- Background: ¹/₄ yd of Medium Dark Golden Yellow fabric (Three 4⁷/₈" squares) (Background yardage is for Section D also)
- Background: ¹/₄ yd of Medium Light Golden Yellow fabric (Three 4⁷/₈" squares)
- See Section D for applique materials and instructions

INSTRUCTIONS:
1. Pair a light and dark Golden Yellow fabric square. Place right sides together. Draw a diagonal. Sew ¹/₄" on each side of the line. Cut on the line. Open the square. Press seam toward the darker fabric. Trim to 4¹/₂".
2. See diagram for block assembly.
3. You won't be able to do the applique until the quilt sections are sewn together.

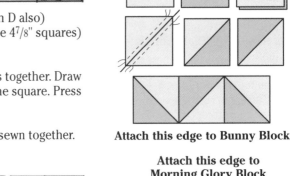

Morning Glory Block Assembly

Attach this edge to Bunny Block

Bunny Block Section C

Finished size: 8¹/₂" x 12¹/₂" (lower section)

MATERIALS:
- Background: ¹/₈ yd each of 3 different Green fabrics labeled A, B, and C. (Includes yardage for Section D)
- White felted wool (12" x 12")
- *DMC* size 8 Ecru Perle cotton or 3 strands embroidery floss
- *DMC* Pink 3 strand embroidery floss for bunny eyes
- *Lite Steam-A-Seam 2* fusible web for applique pieces

INSTRUCTIONS:
1. Cut 2 squares 4¹/₂" from fabrics A, B, and C. Arrange squares using Square Arrangement diagram. Use ¹/₄" seams to piece 2 rows of 3. Press seams in opposite directions on alternating rows.
2. You won't be able to applique the bunny until Section C is sewn to Section A/B Trace 2 bunnies onto fusible web following manufacturer's directions. Fuse and Blanket stitch around the bunny. Stitch a Pink "x" for bunny eyes.

Bunny pattern on page 42.

Attach this edge to Morning Glory Block

A	B	C
C	A	B

Bunny Block Assembly

Holly Berry Block Section C

Finished size: 12¹/₂" x 12¹/₂"

MATERIALS:
- Background: ¹/₈ yd each of 8 Cream and White prints (4¹/₂" x 45") labeled 1-8
- Gold felted wool for flame (2" x 3")
- Dark Red felted wool for candle (2" x 6")
- Dark Green and Medium Green felted wool for leaves (4" x 8" each)
- Red felted wool for berries (5" square)
- *DMC* size 8 Perle cotton or 3 strand embroidery floss to match wool

INSTRUCTIONS:
1. From fabrics 1-8, cut 2¹/₂" squares: 5 from #1, 5 from #2, 5 from #3, 5 from #4, 4 from #5, 4 from #6, 4 from #7, and 4 from #8. You will have 36 squares total.
2. Arrange squares according to the diagram. Use ¹/₄" seams. Stitch vertical columns first. Arrows indicate pressing direction. Sew the columns together.
3. Trace patterns onto freezer paper. Cut a 2" x 6" candle, and 1 flame. Cut 5 Holly leaves and 8 berries from the Table Runner pattern on page 75.
4. Press freezer paper patterns onto wool. Cut out. Blanket stitch in place. Leave candle drips and leaf details for quilting.

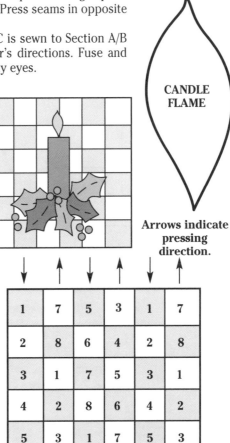

CANDLE FLAME

Arrows indicate pressing direction.

1	7	5	3	1	7
2	8	6	4	2	8
3	1	7	5	3	1
4	2	8	6	4	2
5	3	1	7	5	3
6	4	2	8	6	4

Holly Berry Square Arrangement

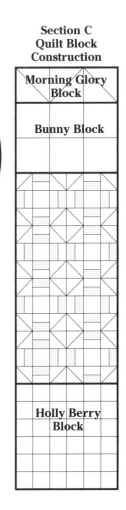

Section C Quilt Block Construction

Morning Glory Block

Bunny Block

Holly Berry Block

Pineapple Block Section C

Finished size: 12$\frac{1}{2}$" x 24$\frac{1}{2}$"

MATERIALS:

- Background: $\frac{1}{4}$ yd each of 2 Tan fabrics, light A and darker B, for half square triangles
- $\frac{1}{8}$ yd each of 2 Tan fabrics, darker C and lighter D, for rectangles
- $\frac{1}{8}$ yd of Tan fabric labeled E for center square
- Gold felted wool (8" x 13")
- Green felted wool (8" x 8")
- *DMC* size 8 Ecru Perle cotton or 3 strands embroidery floss to match wool

INSTRUCTIONS:

1. Cut 2 strips 2$\frac{7}{8}$" x 44" from fabrics A and B. Place strips right sides together, lining up edges. Cut into 16 squares 2$\frac{7}{8}$". Cut each square in half diagonally. Sew a $\frac{1}{4}$" seam along the diagonal cut. Press open. You should have 32 half square triangles that measure 2$\frac{1}{2}$" x 2$\frac{1}{2}$".
2. Cut 2 strips 1$\frac{1}{2}$" x 44" from fabrics C and D. Place strips right sides together, lining up edges. Use $\frac{1}{4}$" seams to sew one long edge. Press seam toward the darker fabric. Cut into 2$\frac{1}{2}$" squares.
3. Cut fabric E into 8 squares 2$\frac{1}{2}$" x 2$\frac{1}{2}$".
4. Arrange pieces according to the Block Construction diagram. Make 4 of each block.
5. See Block placement diagram. Sew 4 rows of 2. Press seams in opposite directions on alternating rows.
6. Trace the pineapple and leaf onto the freezer paper. Cut out and press to the wool. Cut out shapes. Baste in place. Blanket stitch around appliques. Save the diagonal lines and "x's" in the pattern for quilting.

Section C Quilt Block Construction

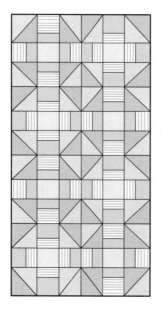

Block Construction Diagrams

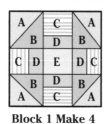

Block 1 Make 4   Block 2 Make 4

Block Placement Diagram

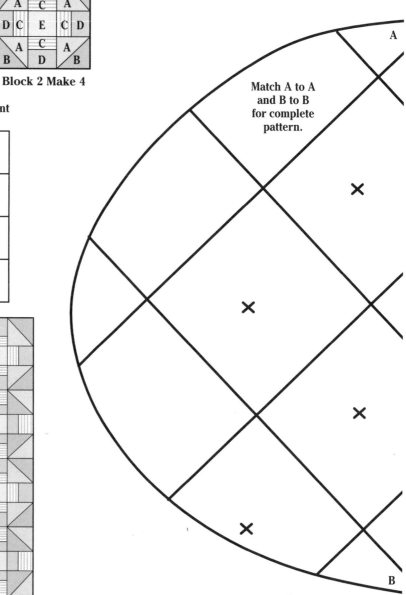

Match A to A and B to B for complete pattern.

Seasonal Delights Quilt

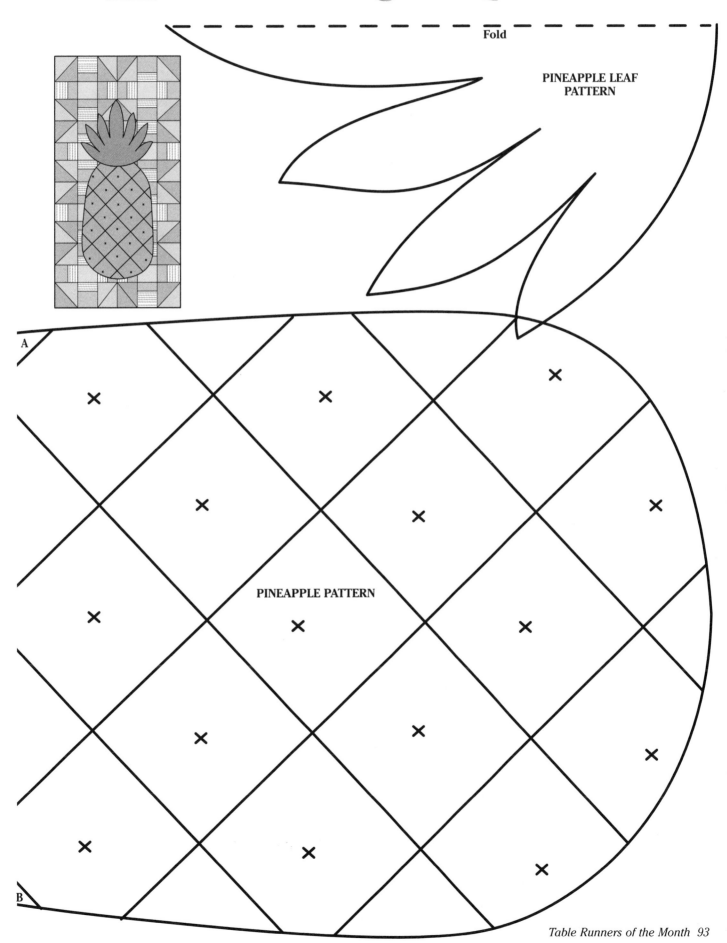

Fold

PINEAPPLE LEAF PATTERN

A

PINEAPPLE PATTERN

B

Snowflake Block Section D

Finished Size: 12$\frac{1}{2}$" x 16$\frac{1}{2}$"

MATERIALS:
- Background: $\frac{1}{8}$ yd of 3 Blue print fabrics referred to as fabrics A, B, and C
- 1 piece White felted wool for snowflakes (8" x 11")
- *DMC* Light Blue size 8 Perle cotton or 2 strands embroidery floss
- Lite Steam-A-Seam 2 fusible web

INSTRUCTIONS:
1. Cut 4 squares 4$\frac{1}{2}$" from fabrics A, B, and C.
2. Trace snowflake patterns on fusible web, following manufacturer's directions. Cut out on the drawn line.
3. Arrange 4$\frac{1}{2}$" squares according to diagram. Sew together in 3 rows using a $\frac{1}{4}$" seam. Press. Sew rows together. Press.
4. Position and Blanket stitch snowflakes on background one at a time. If fusing, use a press cloth to protect wool.

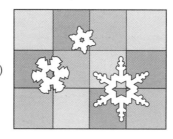

Snowflake patterns on pages 32-33.

Block Arrangement

A	B	C	A
B	C	A	B
C	A	B	C

Applique Arrangement

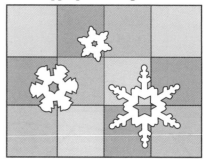

Section D Quilt Block Construction

Snowflake Block   Morning Glory Block   Bunny Block

Bunny Block for Section D

Finished size: 7$\frac{1}{2}$" x 14$\frac{1}{2}$"

MATERIALS:
- Background: Two 4$\frac{1}{2}$" squares from 4 different Green fabrics (Refer to yardage on Section C)
- White felted wool (12" x 12")
- *DMC* size 8 Ecru Perle cotton or 3 strands embroidery floss
- *DMC* Pink 3 strand embroidery floss for bunny eyes

INSTRUCTIONS:
1. See Square Arrangement diagram. Use $\frac{1}{4}$" seams to piece background Green fabrics in 2 rows of 4. Press seams in opposite directions on alternating rows.
2. You won't be able to applique the bunny until the sections are sewn together. Trace a bunny pattern on freezer paper and transfer to wool. Cut out bunny and Blanket stitch around the bunny. Stitch a Pink "x" for bunny eyes.

Bunny pattern on page 42.

Square Arrangement Diagram

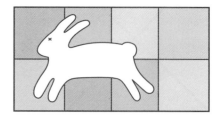

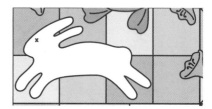

Seasonal Delights Quilt

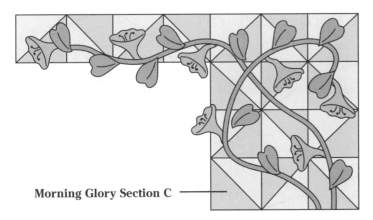

Morning Glory Section C

Morning Glory Block Assembly

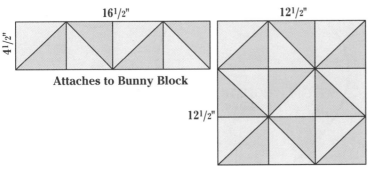

16¹/₂"

4¹/₂"

Attaches to Bunny Block

12¹/₂"

12¹/₂"

Attaches to Morning Glory Section C

Morning Glory Blocks for Section D

Finished size: 4¹/₂" x 16¹/₂"; 12¹/₂" x 12¹/₂" (upper rows)

MATERIALS:
- Background: Seven 4⁷/₈" squares of Medium Dark Golden fabric (See Section C for yardage)
- Background: Seven 4⁷/₈" squares of Medium Light Golden fabric (See Section C for yardage) Yellow fabric ()
- Green and Blue felted wool for leaves and flowers: (6" x 14" each)
- 1 fat quarter Green homespun for stems: (18" x 22")
- *DMC* size 8 Perle cotton or 3 strands embroidery floss to match appliques

INSTRUCTIONS:
1. Pair a light and dark Golden Yellow fabric square. Place right sides together. Draw a diagonal. Sew ¹/₄" on each side of the line. Cut on the line. Open the square. Press seam toward the darker fabric. Trim to 4¹/₂".
2. See diagram for block assembly.
3. You won't be able to do the applique until the quilt sections are sewn together. Trace 11 Green leaves and 7 Blue flowers onto freezer paper. Cut out shapes and press to wool. Cut ³/₄" bias strips from Green homespun. Fold and press. Blanket stitch vines, flowers and leaves in place.

Morning Glory patterns on page 39.

SECTION D: PRESS AFTER EACH SEAM.
1. Sew the Morning Glory to the Bunny block.
2. Sew the Snowflake block to step 1.
3. Sew the Morning Glories square to Step 2.
4. Sew Step 3 to Quilt section A/B/C.
5. Finish applique as needed.
Quilt measures 44¹/₂" x 60¹/₂".

"Remember the 'galloping pony' rule: If you can't see it (a mistake) from a galloping pony, it's probably OK."
Betty Edgell

Seasonal Delights Quilt

Hollyhock Border Patterns

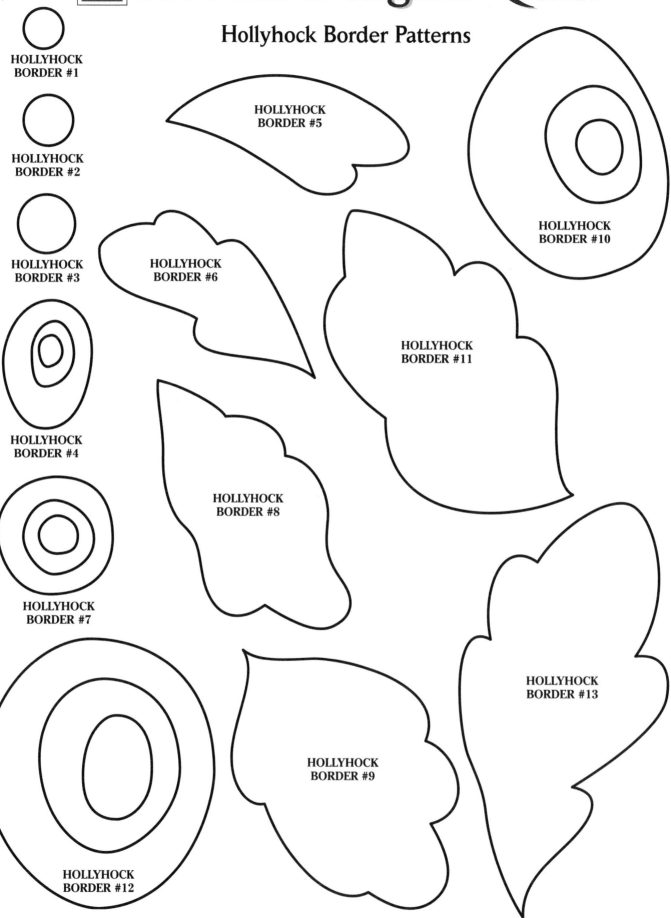

HOLLYHOCK BORDER #1

HOLLYHOCK BORDER #2

HOLLYHOCK BORDER #3

HOLLYHOCK BORDER #4

HOLLYHOCK BORDER #5

HOLLYHOCK BORDER #6

HOLLYHOCK BORDER #7

HOLLYHOCK BORDER #8

HOLLYHOCK BORDER #9

HOLLYHOCK BORDER #10

HOLLYHOCK BORDER #11

HOLLYHOCK BORDER #12

HOLLYHOCK BORDER #13

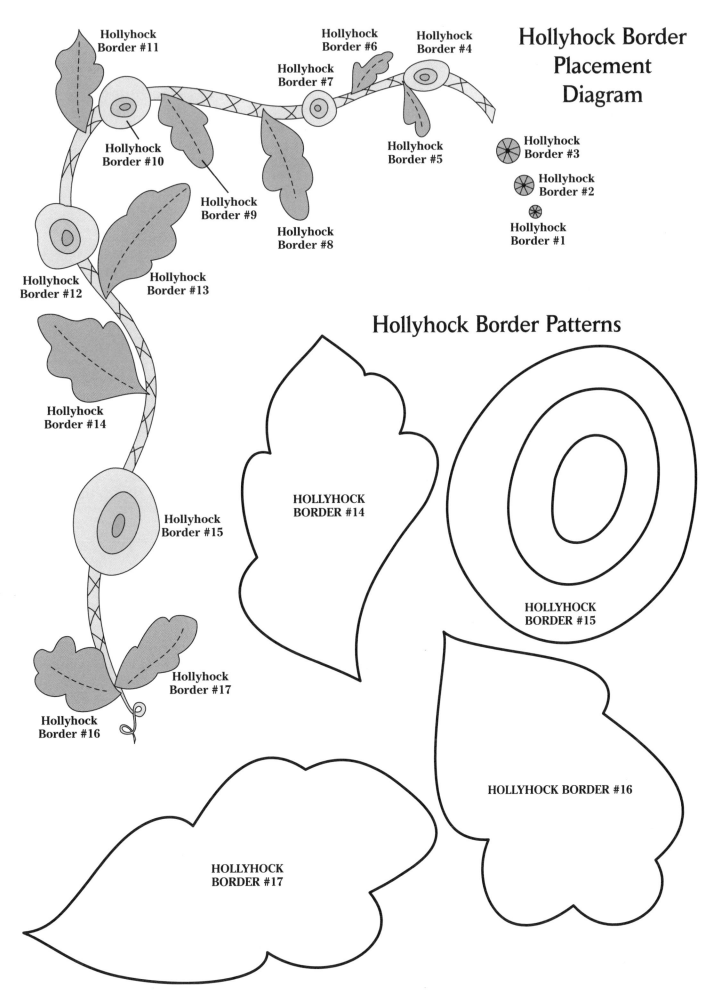

Hollyhock Border Placement Diagram

Hollyhock Border #11

Hollyhock Border #6

Hollyhock Border #4

Hollyhock Border #7

Hollyhock Border #10

Hollyhock Border #5

Hollyhock Border #3

Hollyhock Border #9

Hollyhock Border #2

Hollyhock Border #8

Hollyhock Border #1

Hollyhock Border #12

Hollyhock Border #13

Hollyhock Border #14

Hollyhock Border #15

Hollyhock Border #17

Hollyhock Border #16

Hollyhock Border Patterns

HOLLYHOCK BORDER #14

HOLLYHOCK BORDER #15

HOLLYHOCK BORDER #16

HOLLYHOCK BORDER #17

Embroidery Stitches

Working with Floss.

Separate embroidery floss. • Use 24" lengths of floss and a #8 embroidery needle. • Use 2 to 3 ply floss to outline large elements of the design and to embroider larger and more stylized patterns. • Use 2 ply for the small details on some items.

Blanket Stitch

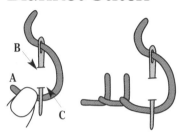

Come up at A, hold the thread down with your thumb, go down at B. Come back up at C with the needle tip over the thread. Pull the stitch into place. Repeat, outlining with the bottom legs of the stitch. Use this stitch to edge fabrics.

Chain Stitch

Come up at A. To form a loop, hold the thread down with your thumb, go down at B (as close as possible to A). Come back up at C with the needle tip over the thread. Repeat to form a chain.

Cross Stitch

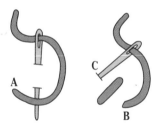

Make a diagonal Straight stitch (up at A, down at B) from upper right to lower left. Come up at C and go down at D to make another diagonal Straight stitch the same length as the first one. The stitch will form an X.

French Knot

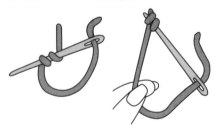

Come up at A. Wrap the floss around the needle 2 to 3 times. Insert the needle close to A. Hold the floss and pull the needle through the loops gently.

Pay attention to backgrounds.

When working with lighter-colored fabrics, do not carry dark flosses across large unworked background areas. Stop and start again to prevent unsightly 'ghost strings' from showing through the front. OR back tinted muslin with another layer of muslin before embroidering. This will help keep 'ghost strings' from showing.

Running Stitch

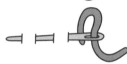

Come up at A. Weave the needle through the fabric, making short, even stitches. Use this stitch to gather fabrics, too.

Satin Stitch

Work small straight stitches close together and at the same angle to fill an area with stitches. Vary the length of the stitches as required to keep the outline of the area smooth.

Stem Stitch

Work from left to right to make regular, slanting stitches along the stitch line. Bring the needle up above the center of the last stitch. Also called 'Outline' stitch.

Straight Stitch

Come up at A and go down at B to form a simple flat stitch. Use this stitch for hair for animals and for simple petals on small flowers.

Whip Stitch

Insert needle under a few fibers of one layer of fabric. Bring needle up through other layer of fabric. Use this stitch to attach the folded raw edges of fabric to back of pieces or to attach bindings around edges of quilts and coverlets.

SUPPLIERS - Most craft and variety stores carry an excellent assortment of supplies. If you need something special, ask your local store to contact the following companies:

LITE STEAM-A-SEAM
   The Warm Company, 800-234-WARM, Seattle, WA
PERLE COTTON AND EMBROIDERY FLOSS
   DMC, 973-589-0606, S. Kearny, NJ
RIBBON
   Offray, 908-879-4700, Chester, NJ
BOHIN SHARPS NEEDLES
   United Notions, 800-527-9447, Dallas, TX
TABLE RUNNER KITS
   Lone Star House of Quilts, 817-277-4749, Arlington, TX
   www.lonestarhouseofquilts.com

SPECIAL THANKS to: Alice and Dave Cooksey at Lone Star House of Quilts for their encouragement and support in our creative endeavor; to Garland Edgell for his computer expertise; to our husbands (Steve Chutchian, Garland Edgell, Andrew Lester) for their patience and encouragement; to Karen Roxbourgh of Karen's Kreative Quilting for her outstanding quilting talent.

- Betsy, Betty and Judith

Thanks also to: Kathy McMillan; Jennifer Laughlin
Charlie Davis Young; Patty Williams; Marti Wyble;
Donna Kinsey; David & Donna Thomason